D1611413

Counternarratives from Women of Color Academics

This book documents the lived experiences of women of color academics who have leveraged their professional positions to challenge the status quo in academia through their scholarship, teaching, service, activism, and leadership. By presenting reflexive work from various vantage points within and outside of the academy, contributors document the cultivation of mentoring relationships, the use of administrative roles to challenge institutional leadership, and more. Through an emphasis on the various ways in which women of color have succeeded in the academy—albeit with setbacks along the way—this volume aims to change the discourse surrounding women of color academics: from a focus on trauma and mere survival to a focus on courage and thriving.

Manya C. Whitaker is an assistant professor of Education at Colorado College, USA.

Eric Anthony Grollman is an assistant professor of Sociology at the University of Richmond, USA.

Routledge Research in Higher Education

For more information about this series, please visit: www.routledge.com/
Routledge-Research-in-Higher-Education/book-series/RRHE

Counternarratives from Women of Color Academics

Bravery, Vulnerability, and Resistance

Edited by Manya C. Whitaker
and Eric Anthony Grollman

NEW YORK AND LONDON

First published 2019
by Routledge
711 Third Avenue, New York, NY 10017

and by Routledge
2 Park Square, Milton Park, Abingdon, Oxon, OX14 4RN

Routledge is an imprint of the Taylor & Francis Group, an informa business

© 2019 Taylor & Francis

Library of Congress Cataloguing-in-Publication Data
A catalog record for this book has been requested

ISBN: 978-1-138-61090-3 (hbk)
ISBN: 978-0-429-46550-5 (ebk)

Typeset in Sabon
by Apex CoVantage, LLC

For every woman of color in the academy, especially the ones who have not yet recognized their bravery.

Contents

Foreword

Bianca C. Williams

A few months ago, I sat in a café in Brooklyn, NY, listening to one of my sista scholars[1] offer remarks at the celebration of my first book, *The Pursuit of Happiness: Black Women, Diasporic Dreams, and the Politics of Emotional Transnationalism*. My family and friends filled the room, and I sat in a chair soaking up every word as she described our process of becoming friends and sista scholars. Her students had already read some chapters of the book and she provided their feedback, detailing how they connected with the Black women in my ethnography on happiness, travel, and diaspora. Her remarks ended with gratitude: "Thank you for putting this book out into the world. Thank you for putting so much of yourself out into the world. I see you. I hear you. I appreciate you. I love you." A whirlwind of intense emotions floated through my body as I tried to take in her accolades and the special moment. There was laughter and a few tears. I was somewhat in disbelief that I had made it to this side of the academic process: I am an author; I am tenured; and, I am a Black feminist anthropologist. I teach, I organize, I write, and I manage to do it without losing my voice or myself.

A year and a half before this celebration, I was in the middle of one of the toughest fights of my life. I was in a tenure battle in which some members of my department (folx I believed to be part of my community) were my greatest nemeses. I was struggling with writing anxiety as I completed the final revisions of the book. And I was a co-founder and co-lead for my city's chapter of Black Lives Matter, where we worked day and night collaborating with members of our community to organize against police violence. Of course, this took a toll not only on my professional life, but also on my personal relationships and my physical, emotional, and spiritual wellness. I felt broken. I was discouraged and tired. I couldn't see past these tribulations to envision what life could be like afterwards, as I could barely pull myself together to fight the battles at hand. I knew about the powerful stories and useful analyses of women of color in books like *Presumed Incompetent* and *Written/unwritten*, and they helped me not feel alone. But during that time, I would've loved to have a book such as the one you are currently holding. The stories of bravery, vulnerability, and multiple forms of resistance offered in this text would have provided some needed solace and hope.

Counternarratives from Women of Color Academics: Bravery, Vulnerability, and Resistance is the pep talk, the brainstorming of practical strategies, the motivating force we all need when the academy has us down—those moments when we have to be brave. This book is full of narratives from women of color academics who endured the course and made it through various types of fire. Here, they share their stories not only of survival, but of thriving after adversity. Not all chose to stay in the academy; some decided that their path to triumph led them to be brave truth-telling resisters in other spaces and manifestations. However, each person has an offering useful for those times when we are reminded that these institutions were not made for us, and that *la lucha* (the fight) for equity, visibility, and respect continues.

Many texts on women of color in the academy document and theorize the oppressive forces that influence our academic and professional careers. This research is necessary for producing structural change that will lead to long-term transformation in educational institutions. However, sometimes we, and these texts, center the mechanisms of our disenfranchisement so much that we don't take the time to recognize and celebrate the ways we still succeed and win despite these forces. Instead of starting from a deficit-perspective, *Counternarratives from Women of Color Academics* speaks about our gifts, skills, innovation, discipline- and institution-building abilities, and our legacy of creating amazing careers in spaces that continue to try to exclude us.

Many of us do research on communities that are marginalized because we understand that by centering them we can often get the most holistic view of the factors at play in whichever phenomena we are studying. Those who are alienated, kept at the bottom of a hierarchy, or pushed to the margins, must grasp how things work in order to survive, thrive, and resist. Their lives often depend on this awareness and analysis. They are also the ones who have spent some time dreaming up alternatives, inventing new strategies, and building relationships that push tradition and lead to innovation. This wealth of knowledge that marginalized folx have holds true for women of color academics, including the contributors to this book. And institutions truly interested in diversity, equality, and equity would do well to seek and value this knowledge.

Each chapter illustrates the power of vulnerability, and the transformative work that can be done when we refuse to be silent about who we are, about what we've been through, about how we feel as we fight. Here, the poems and essays point to the numerous styles, tongues, and ways we speak our truths. The chapters are in conversation with one another, bursting with examples of women of color showing up for themselves and each other, providing support, making one another visible, mirroring and affirming, organizing, advocating, and refusing to play it safe. As individuals, and as a collective, when women of color speak up, act up, live to fight another day, things change. These authors take adversity and turn it into hard-won, sometimes soul-trying victories, while also teaching others how to win through their lessons learned. When one of us gets through the door, we not only leave the door open, but try to provide guidance to make getting through the door easier.

It's a familiar experience for many women of color academics. Whether it is during office hours, in the halls at conferences, or over drinks after the business meeting, someone is going to ask you how you made it through. How did you succeed in undergrad? How did you make it through your research project and defend the dissertation? How do you thrive in the class-room? Is it possible to be a scholar-activist? What does it take to get the tenure-track position? Write the book? Become an administrator? Create that research center? Lead that professional organization? How did you do all that within the context of racism and sexism? Can you teach me? As you take a deep breath and open up your soul to tell them about your journey, a range of emotions frequently show up.

In the past, when overwhelmed with everything I wanted to offer in these conversations, I would often point students and peers to *Conditionally Accepted*, the blog founded by Eric Anthony Grollman (a co-editor of this book). The blog was one of the few digital spaces where I felt that academics of color were able to bring their whole selves to the conversation and share narratives that provided insight into how we could make it the other side of adversity. The radical honesty and dedication to practicing intersectional and inclusive politics Eric and other blog contributors displayed was power-ful. And no one I ever sent to it walked away without learning something useful. I came across Manya Whitaker's work (the other co-editor of this book) for the first time through *Conditionally Accepted*, after the blog gen-erated significant traffic as a regular career advice column for *Inside Higher Ed* in January 2016. Manya's ability to combine her personal narrative with scholarly research findings made her one of my favorite contributors, while her practical strategies for leaving your mark on the academy also stood out. As co-editors of this book, Manya and Eric have produced a text that carries forth the truth-telling of *Conditionally Accepted*. Significantly, they did not wait until tenure to be brave, vulnerable, and resistant, and I, for one, am very grateful.

We need books like this. We need spaces where we can be brave enough not only to tell our stories, but to highlight the ingenious ways that (with our community's help) we beat the odds. Like the fierce, truth-telling pre-decessors who gifted us books such as *But Some of Us Are Brave*, and *Still Brave*, Manya, Eric, and the contributors are providing narratives that will help us make it through. Now, when people ask you how you made it through adversity, you can share your story and send them a copy of this book. Let them know that they are connected to a community of women of color academics who are ready to celebrate their victories.

To the women of color who poured their hearts into writing each chapter, and to the editors who saw this labor of love through each stage of production, "Thank you for putting this book out into the world. Thank you for putting so much of yourself out into the world. I see you. I hear you. I appreciate you."

In Solidarity,
Bianca C. Williams

Note

1 Gratitude to Dr. Ashanté Reese for her practice of sisterhood, and for permission to share her kind words.

Preface

A Note from Manya

When Eric and I initially decided to do an anthology that celebrated women of color academics, I saw it as an opportunity to participate in an important discussion. I was tired of discourse that paints us as hostile and difficult to work with, when in fact, we are probably the demographic most easy to work with because we've *had* to figure out how to make it work. Despite misogyny, racism, and classism, women of color academics continue to succeed in the academy. That's the story I wanted to tell.

My second motivation for editing *Counternarratives from Women of Color Academics* was about discourse between women of color. A couple of years ago I realized how draining it is to have conversation after conversation about the perils of being a woman, being of color, and especially being a woman of color working in a white male-dominated space. In my real life and in my online life, women of color seemed to be talking only about the trauma we've endured at the hands of white men and women (and sometimes, other women of color). It really hit home after I read *Presumed Incompetent*. I couldn't finish the book because it was just too real. Story after story of struggle made me realize that women of color need to share their stories of thrival, too.

That's what *Counternarratives* is for.

From day one of this project I was forced to confront just how many of us have been so beaten down that we consider just showing up to work a success within itself. And I agree. But my hope is that this book will push you to recognize and honor how women of color academics do more than show up. We resist, we fight, and we win.

And through our collective bravery, we will have freedom.

Because as Nina Simone said, freedom is no fear.

A Note from Eric

My earliest exposure to the awe-inspiring bravery of women of color in the face of systemic oppression, crushing poverty, and violence was my mother's journey. She is one of eight children from a poor, single-parent family. Later in life, while working full-time and raising me, she successfully obtained an associate's degree, then a bachelor's degree, and then a master's degree. Her courage, as I observed it over the years, was daring to pursue success and luxuries unknown not only to her relatives, but also generations of ancestors before her. It was her refusal to be defined by the circumstances into which she was born, as well as the low expectations others held for her simply because of her race, gender, and social class. It was refusing to give up just because it was hard, or because she experienced pushback and even discrimination, or because she lacked role models who looked like her. She has granted me permission to publish her poem about her perseverance and bravery:

If I Never Try...

> If I never take the initiative,
> Then I'll never know real courage or find victory in defeat.
> If I never challenge myself and strive to do more,
> Then I'll never know my own strength or how to endure.
> If I never demand more and keep settling for less,
> Then I'll never know my true value, riches or success.
> If I never speak out against hurts and continue to suffer in shame,
> Then I'll always be treated shabbily and should expect more of the
>   same.
> If I never love myself and have little self-esteem,
> Then how can I expect others to love me and welcome me as part of
>   the team?
> If I never have before, God, please help me learn before I die,
> That nothing beats a failure, except the effort to at least try.
>
> *By Cynthia Cox-Grollman*
> *March 1998*

I've long known of the fearlessness of women of color. But it was only recently that I decided to create whatever platform I could to celebrate their bravery. The seed was planted as I sat on a 2015 Parren Mitchell panel on intellectual activism at the University of Maryland. One of my fellow panelists, Dr. Brittney Cooper, shared the following insight: "I think that there's far too much *intellectual cowardice* in the academy. Right, which is to say, that folks see injustices going down, and they won't say anything about it."

I began to take stock of those whom I considered the risk-takers and the trailblazers. I saw unapologetic scholar-activists like Drs. Cooper, Patricia Hill Collins, Anthea Butler, Tamura Lomax, and others continuing a long tradition of Black women's intellectual activism. I was inspired by women of color scholars like Drs. Kerry Ann Rockquemore, Fatimah Williams Castro, Bedelia Richards, and Manya C. Whitaker, who launched their own businesses. I observed women of color scholars who refused to be silenced, be defined by others, be constrained by mainstream norms about what an academic should do and should value.

This collaborative project with Manya and all of our contributing authors is truly a labor of love. We worked hard to create this gift—a celebration of the limitless courage of women of color in the academy and beyond. While marginalization and trauma are, unfortunately, inevitable consequences of academic life for women of color, we are committed to a new vision of the positive aspects that often go overlooked: bravery, thrival, and self-definition. We hope that this snapshot of the lives of current scholars will inspire future generations of women of color.

Women of color academics: we see you. We celebrate you. We love you.

Acknowledgments

As the two of us live on opposites sides of the country and work in different disciplines, we would be remiss if we did not thank Dr. CJ Pascoe, who had the insight to introduce us to one another and help two kindred spirits meet. This anthology would also not have been possible without the generous advice of colleagues who had published one or more of their own anthologies on marginalized academics: Drs. Patricia A. Matthews, Brian L. McGowan, Kristine De Welde, Andi Stepnick, Gabriella Gutiérrez y Muhs, Yolanda Flores Niemann, Carmen G. González, Angela P. Harris, and especially Dwayne Mack. And we appreciate the encouragement and guidance of Matthew Friberg, our editor at Routledge/Taylor & Francis, throughout the process of editing and publishing this book.

Manya & Eric

I never saw myself co-editing an anthology, especially not as pre-tenure faculty. Indeed, I give credit to Eric Anthony Grollman (they/them/theirs) for having the nerve to even dream of such a text, and the tenacity to enact their vision. I extend to them my gratitude for inviting me to participate in such a worthwhile project. I had the courage to accept Eric's invitation because of two senior women colleagues of color at Colorado College: Dr. Claire Garcia and Dr. Adrienne Seward. These women welcomed me into academia when I was brand new and had no idea what it would be like as one of four Black women at a predominately white institution. They modeled how to advocate for myself and for others, no matter the professional consequences. I am grateful for their mentorship and support, and for all they risked so that I could have a place at the table. I am similarly indebted to my mother, Linda Whitaker, whose endless belief that I can do anything instilled in me the confidence to step out on faith and edit this anthology. Finally, I thank the twenty-six contributors to *Counternarratives* for being brave enough to be vulnerable as we collectively resist.

Manya C. Whitaker

The courage it took to pursue a project like *Counternarratives*, especially while on the tenure-track (when I "should" be publishing "real" research), did not come from me alone. That courage was deeply influenced by several people in my life, in both personal and professional capacities. I am grateful to my maternal grandmother Barbara Cox, my maternal aunt Dannette Jones, and, most of all, my mother Cynthia A. Cox-Grollman—three Black women who have spoken out against injustice and advocated for oppressed people, planting the seeds for my own bravery and commitment to Black feminist politics. I am also grateful to my paternal grandfather Sylvan Grollman, my father Elliott Grollman, and my partner Eric Knauff—three white men who have encouraged me to pursue and value happiness and authenticity. I must thank my co-conspirators at ConditionallyAccepted.com— Drs. Victor Ray, Jeana Jorgensen, J. E. Sumerau, Jackson Wright Shultz and, of course, Manya C. Whitaker; we knew a book like *Counternarratives* was the inevitable next step to our blog. Several colleagues at the University of Richmond have encouraged me to be my authentic scholar-activist self, including Drs. Bedelia Richards, Patricia Herrera, Andrea Simpson, Mari Lee Misfud, Erika Zimmerman Damer, April Hill, Paul Achter, Kathleen Roberts Skerrett, Del McWhorter, Jane Geaney, Malcolm Hill, and Libby Gruner. Major thanks go to my accountability partner and good friend, Dr. Krystale Littlejohn, who has been a lifeline for me as I struggle to navigate mental health struggles, tenure stress, and the tension between activism and academia. And thanks to Dr. Juhi Verma who helped to spark my interest in documenting the stories of brave women of color academics. Most of all, I am grateful to Dr. Manya C. Whitaker—my co-editor, friend, co-conspirator, and ally—for taking this journey with me. I could not, and would not, have done this project without you, Manya!

Eric Anthony Grollman

1 Introduction

Manya C. Whitaker and
Eric Anthony Grollman

This anthology is a celebration. It is a celebration of the women of color in academia who refuse to play it safe, who define what it means to be a scholar on their own terms, and who challenge the status quo within, and outside of, the ivory tower. This collection of original essays and creative works represents our effort to recognize and honor the bravery, vulnerability, and resistance embodied and enacted by women of color academics in their scholarship, teaching, mentorship, service, activism, and leadership.

We have two main goals for the anthology. First, we aim to change the discourse surrounding the professional and personal experiences of women of color academics from conversations about mere *survival* to a celebration of *thrival*. Since the 1982 publication of the pivotal text *But Some of Us Are Brave: Black Women's Studies*, at least two dozen anthologies on the experiences of women of color in the academy have been published. These texts, including the very popular 2012 anthology, *Presumed Incompetent: The Intersections of Race and Class for Women Academics*, do the essential task of naming the harsh realities of racist, sexist, and classist discrimination, harassment, and microaggressions that women of color face on a daily basis in academia. However, the preponderance of stories of victimization and marginalization have painted a rather bleak picture. Accounts of tokenism, isolation, marginalization, exclusion, and other manifestations of oppression are only one part of the story for women of color in academia. Through *Counternarratives*, we aim to tell another key part of their stories. In particular, we aim to shift the narrative from victimization to empowerment, from inauthenticity to self-definition, and from conformity to resistance.

Our second goal is to challenge the dominant definition of success in the academy. As our contributors and many other marginalized scholars know first-hand, the academy privileges the interests, needs, and experiences of middle- and upper-class white heterosexual cisgender men without disabilities. Even when we attempt to succeed by their rules, we come up short. The essays in this anthology confront the norms about what it means to be a successful academic, including how we dress, speak, and behave, the topics we study, the research methods we use, and how and what we teach. In many cases, the authors offer concrete strategies for effectively challenging the status quo while guarding against the penalties of such actions in the academy. It is our hope to celebrate the indomitable spirit of 21st-century women of color academics, and to inspire the next generation of women of color scholars and scholar-activists to be both brave and vulnerable as they resist the outdated and exclusive norms of the ivory tower.

Methodology

In June 2016, we widely distributed a call for essays and creative works for an anthology about academic bravery, inviting women of every racial and ethnic minority group in the US to contribute. We emphasized our desire to include the voices of women of color from intersections that are too often overlooked, namely LGBTQ women of color, women of color with disabilities, immigrant women of color, and first-generation and work-ing-class women of color. We welcomed women of color academics from every academic discipline and career stage, as well as minority women in contingent faculty positions, and those who pursued non-academic careers. Our goal was not to tokenize women of color academics from various backgrounds; rather, we knew there was much to learn from the lived experiences of women of color from every intersectional social location.

We were pleased to receive nearly 350 submissions of essays, poems, photographs, plays, and paintings from women of color academics around the country. The sheer volume of submissions proved daunting to evaluate one by one. And we also found the process of reading these submissions emotionally taxing, even depressing at times. Many, or perhaps even most, of the submissions featured narratives of trauma rather than the stories of resilience, resistance, courage, and authenticity we'd hoped to read. The overwhelming tales of pain and disappointment made us more certain that an anthology that centers happiness and serenity was essential for the heal-ing and continued success of women of color academics in the US. In the end, we selected the twenty-nine abstracts that told stories of triumph—big or small, personal or professional—from which other women of color aca-demics could seek inspiration or guidance.

Once accepted, we encouraged our contributors to use a personal, rather than scholarly, approach to telling their stories. If they were to sit down with a friend, mentee, or colleague, how would they tell their tales? What advice would they give? You will see that citations of academic literature are minimal, with some essays using none at all. We asked our contributors to let their own descriptions serve as evidence of their bravery, vulnerabil-ity, and resistance. In that vein, we echo the critical race and critical race feminist emphasis on storytelling, as well as the Latina feminist practice of *testimonio*, as forms of knowledge-production about the lived experiences of women of color (Delgado & Stefancic, 2012; The Latina Feminist Group, 2001; Wing, 2003).

For contributors unfamiliar with such emotive forms of writing, we suggested they utilize the Scholarly Personal Narrative (SPN) approach articulated by Robert J. Nash in his 2004 book, *Liberating Scholarly Writing: The Power of Personal Narrative*. Nash developed the SPN methodology as an alternative to traditional academic writing, which forces marginalized scholars to suppress their humanity and emotions in the face of oppression. Instead, he offers SPN as a liberatory writing praxis focused on self-reflection, self-discovery, and self-growth.

It became apparent throughout the revision process that few, if any, of our contributors had prior experience with the SPN method. Some essays underwent as many as four rounds of substantial revision because many authors struggled with personal meaning-making. Having to articulate what about their decision-making or actions demonstrated bravery, vulnerability, and/or resistance proved somewhat challenging. Some authors admitted that they did not really know *why* they acted in a certain way at the time, just that they *had* to act. Others struggled to even name themselves as brave or to claim their own inherent bravery, explaining that bravery was akin to boastfulness or arrogance in their culture. To us, their hesitation to identify and explicitly name positive attributes about themselves echoed how the academy and society consistently demean and devalue women, particularly women of color. This only further proved the urgency of our anthology.

We are therefore grateful to the twenty-six women who stuck with us as we attempted to create a space for narratives about and for women of color academics that does not publicly exist. We are pleased that our contributors span the academic range from PhD student to administrator, with a few who have left the academy. There is representation across disciplinary fields, including English, psychology, political science, sociology, education, women's and gender studies, ethnic studies, theater, anthropology, and engineering. And our contributors come from diverse racial, ethnic, nationality, sexual, and cultural backgrounds. True to our initial goals, there is no singular voice, as "woman of color" is not a monolithic category.

The twenty-one essays and poems herein—roughly 5 percent of the large pool of submissions we initially received—reflect the emotional labor of our contributors who courageously use their voice within a world that prefers they remain silent.

Organization

In Part I of the book, "Resisting Convention: Counternarratives to Conventional Norms and Practices in the Academy," we feature essays by women of color who have bucked the dominant norms of the academy. Some of the authors reflect on strategies they have used to leverage their professional position to create change on campus and beyond. Others discuss their refusal to remain silent in the face of injustice, no matter the consequences. Still others share their courageous decision to leave the academy all together, finding that the profession stifles, rather than fosters, their creativity, passion, and commitment to racial, gender, and economic justice. These authors demonstrate the heights women of color can reach in and beyond the ivory tower when they are bold enough to go against the grain.

Part II of the anthology, "Collective Resistance: Counternarratives to the Ethos of Individualistic Meritocracy in the Academy," presents narratives of women of color academics who resist the American ideal of individualism. Despite this norm, these women work with their mentors and mentees, students and teachers, colleagues, and friends to ensure their own and each other's personal and professional advancement. They create or transform interpersonal spaces within academia to collectively work toward their goals of success, community well-being, and social justice. They subvert the common conception that bravery means overcoming obstacles without help from others; rather, they draw from traditions in communities of color to "lift as they climb."

The third and final part, "Embodied Resistance: Counternarratives to Hegemonic Identities in the Academy," includes essays by women of color academics who do something that many find counterintuitive: harnessing their bravery by being vulnerable. These women describe their intentional efforts to undermine middle- and upper-class white masculinist norms of professionalism in US higher education. While the common view is that vulnerability is a form of weakness, these women articulate that the most courageous thing you can do is expose the most intimate, delicate parts of yourself in a cold, impersonal context. These contributors literally use their bodies as sites of resistance against the academic status quo.

We see *Counternarratives from Women of Color Academics* as offering a new perspective of the lives and experiences of women of color in the academy. This anthology is not an attack on academia nor a call to transform it, per se. Our intention is to recognize and celebrate a little-known fact in our profession: there are many women of color who are doing more than barely surviving—some are actually thriving. However, we also do not intend to paint an unrealistic, rosy picture of the experiences of a select few women of color in the academy. The stories in the following pages are not necessarily happy endings, but they do an excellent job of documenting and celebrating journeys of overcoming, speaking up, and owning your personhood.

As we said at the beginning of this introduction, this is a celebration. Please join us.

References

Delgado, R., & Stefancic, J. (2012). *Critical race theory: An introduction* (2nd ed.). New York, NY: New York University Press.

The Latina Feminist Group. (2001). *Telling to live: Latina feminist* testimonios. Durham, NC: Duke University Press.

Nash, R. J. (2004). *Liberating scholarly writing: The power of personal narrative.* New York, NY: Teachers College Press.

Wing, A. K. (2003). *Critical race feminism: A reader* (2nd ed.). New York, NY: New York University Press.

Part I
Resisting Convention
Counternarratives to Conventional Norms and Practices in the Academy

2 Leading as a Chicana Feminist in a Predominantly White Institution

Yolanda Flores Niemann

My personal, political, and professional identities intersect to form the Chicana feminist and critical race lens from which I served as a formal leader and administrator in academia for sixteen years. To lead through that lens in a predominantly white institution not only takes courage but also requires tenacity, or as one of my mentors called it, "chutzpah"—a slang word that means audacity or nerve.

I identify as a *Tejana*—a descendant of the original Mexican descent persons who lived in Texas while the state was still part of Mexico. The Flores family likes to boast that we have survived all six flags that have flown over Texas: France, Spain, Mexico, Texas, the Confederate States of America, and the United States of America. We did not cross the border, the border crossed *us*. I grew up as the oldest of seven children raised in a family living in very low socioeconomic status—a family that lacked medical care, eventually costing the life of one of my sisters. We often did not know from where our next meal was coming, and we were once evicted for delinquent rent payments. As such, I am very cognizant of power differences resulting from access, authority, and structure. And, as the first in my family to go beyond junior high school, I believe in the transformative power of a formal education to transcend those differences. However, for universities to serve a transformative role for all students, those in formal leadership roles must see beyond the status quo and have the courage to envision and implement institutional and structural change.

Yo soy Chicana—I am a Mexican-American with an activist bent, who takes pride in her racial and ethnic heritage. Chicana feminism informs my values and beliefs. These include: 1) addressing legacies and remnants of historical power, with a focus on the intersections among gender, race, and social class; 2) an understanding that the social construction of race is central to how people of color are constrained in society; 3) a recognition that color-blindness is a fallacy; and 4) an awareness that structural and institutionalized racism persists as a function of the values, policies, and practices that keep members of historically underrepresented groups in subordinate positions. These philosophical beliefs contradict the color-blind neoliberal paradigm of academia in the US today. As such, leading from a Chicana feminist and critical race lens requires constant courage and mindfulness.

Professionally, I am a social psychologist, professor, and scholar who has made a lifelong commitment to studying, teaching, and writing about racism and tokenism in academia, beginning with graduate school exams, thesis, and dissertation. I dedicated my career to identifying, understanding, and eradicating these problems in the field and in the society at large. This pledge stems from my realization that, even in the field of psychology, which intimately serves people of all races and ethnicities, research findings and clinical practice tend to view people of color through a deficit model, negatively comparing us to non-Hispanic white people, who are considered the norm. Choosing to study racism in the face of colleagues and journal reviewers whose views fall along color-blind neoliberalism takes fearlessness and determination. It takes tenacity and a core belief in the importance of speaking truth to power, and of revealing the often hidden truths about elitism and racism in academia, and the damages that can result. Add a tokenized status, wherein I have often been alone to lead fights for justice, an exceptional fortitude is required.

Tokenism typically results from being a member of a group whose numbers are fewer than 15 percent of the total in a role or unit. According to the National Center for Education Statistics (NCES), Latinas certainly fit into tokenized status in academia. In 2013, 77 percent of managers and administrators in higher education were non-Hispanic white men and women; Latina/os were a mere five percent of that total. And, among tenured full professors, 85 percent were white and only 1 percent were Latina. There are real professional and personal consequences to being a token, beyond the scope of this paper (for summaries and discussion see Niemann, 1999, 2003, 2012, 2016). In spite of the token status, I have been able to affect change in various administrative roles—from Special Assistant to the Provost to Senior Vice Provost of Academic Affairs—for students, faculty, and staff. I pursued and implemented change knowing there would be negative personal and professional consequences for going against the status quo, including the loss of a job.

The Courage to Become an Administrator

Upon entering academia, my goal was to become a tenured full professor; I did not plan to become an administrator. However, after a very rough start to my faculty career (see Niemann, "The Making of a Token" 1999), I learned that even tenured senior members of the academy do not necessarily have the courage to go against the status quo; they fear speaking against persons who are more powerful. I wondered how many other faculty of color might be experiencing racism, sexism, and classism, and I was determined to do whatever was in my power to affect structural change and promote equity. I had no idea how to go about obtaining a position of power and authority that would afford me the opportunity to make a difference, but I did have the grit to stand up for the less empowered. As it turned out, my token status in academia facilitated my preparation for administrative leadership.

Because I was always one of the only women of color faculty in the department, college, and/or university, administrators got a "two-fer"—a woman *and* a person of color—by appointing me to committees in which they wanted a "diverse perspective." The heavy service load, while very time- and energy-consuming, gave me insight into the various ways and means of university functions that are not typically transparent to faculty, including behind-the-scenes politics of decision-making and agenda setting. The service work afforded professional development and the opportunity to gain confidence in my administrative and leadership skills. I soon learned, however, that what they wanted by way of diversity in committees was my non-white skin tone, not my Chicana perspective and voice. *But my lens was color-conscious, not color-blind.* Speaking up in these committees, then, often meant going against the intended outcomes pursued by my colleagues and those who convened the committees. That put me at risk of being perceived as an outlier, an outsider, and someone who was not a team player.

As the token person of color in the room, and sometimes the only woman as well, I found myself internally practicing what I wanted to say, and how to say it in a manner that would persuade my counterparts and maintain relationships. I learned to balance the weight of the responsibility for speaking up for the less powerful and underserved with my resolve to lessen the pressure on those who would follow me. My conviction for equity and justice overruled my disquietude, but at the risk of endangering relationships and my career.

I am also a wife and mother, in addition to being the oldest of seven siblings, so I constantly had to balance the emotional energy required for personal and professional needs. This energy was often spent on my advocacy for equity and justice, leaving less time for family. Another price that I paid for engaging in administrative work was that it increasingly took up the finite number of hours and energy in the day. That further removed me from my professional identity and scholarship, which I valued because, through it, I could help women of color at other universities to thrive.

Still, administration began to feel like a calling. With so few Latina full professors in research institutions, and even fewer in administration, my voice mattered. I allowed my administrative voice to grow stronger and braver while I continued to find some time to write, including finishing the path-breaking 2012 anthology, *Presumed Incompetent: The Intersections of Race and Class for Women in Academia.* A few key allies, white and of color, who were in positions to help my advancement, appreciated my unique insight, even when I disagreed with them; they nominated me for upper-level administrative positions.

My experience and training cemented my understanding that administrators are expected to maintain existing power structures, and that those who deviate from the norm put their careers at risk. So, although I had not yet made full professor, I entered formal administrative roles the same week that I was notified that I was awarded tenure, knowing the risk and challenge ahead for a Latina who leads from my critical Chicana lens. I also knew, however, that unless we have a seat at the table and use it to make the most of our voice and actions, nothing changes.

The jobs were lonely. Because the overwhelming majority of my administrative colleagues were white persons who came from a neoliberal, color-blind lens, I could not expect to get support on matters of racial, gender, or socioeconomic justice from them. And I really couldn't discuss confidential matters with anyone else. I dealt with the isolation by forming alliances with women of color and other brave persons who were willing to challenge the status quo in academia. These included a few white insiders who *publicly* shared my views, and other faculty, staff, and students of color across rank, whose support bolstered my courage to continue the administrative road less taken (by choice or by lack of opportunity) by people of color. I scheduled time to maintain relationships with loved ones who valued me for who I am.

Changing the Conversation When Those in Power Shape and Maintain the Conversation

When it comes to faculty evaluation, the general focus of conversation is on what is presumably equal, measured, and quantifiable (e.g., number of publications and grant dollars). That focus on equality excludes what is subjective and equitable, including service performed predominantly by women and people of color. These faculty often get stuck in lower ranks, if they make tenure at all.

To address the inherent inequity in the policies and practices, I developed and led a policy committee of respected full professors from various disciplines and colleges, charging them with clarifying expectations regarding the roles of teaching, research, and service on tenure, promotion, and merit. To that end, I also developed a collaborative partnership with the Faculty Senate Executive Committee. The most controversial part of the policy revision was the inclusion of high levels of service as one path for promotion to full professor. The heavy vetting of the policy across university units revealed problems of inconsistency across campus. It afforded an open discussion of the extent and undervalued role of service performed by women faculty. The service criterion as a path to full professor did not make the final cut for the revised policy, but the discussion did increase awareness of the unequal and extraordinary service conducted by some demographic groups at the expense of their career advancement.

Similarly, to change the conversation about why we lack faculty of color (e.g., "they're just not in the pipeline") in multiple positions that I held, I strongly encouraged deans to change their recruitment strategies. To support them in this endeavor, I developed a major resource list of names, listservs, and websites of faculty of color groups in every field. I used my limited discretionary funds to pay for additional ads in venues that focus on people of color in academia, (e.g., *Hispanic Outlook in Higher Education*). I also provided them with data on the number of PhDs awarded in each field by race and ethnicity. In short, I eliminated excuses for not interviewing faculty of color. Some deans, chairs, and faculty interpreted my efforts as caring only about bringing in faculty of color. They complained and up-line supervisors did not support me. The more pushback I endured, the more indomitable my dedication to affecting change became.

Programs and Safe Spaces When Those in Power Promote Color-Blindness

Having the courage to be a high-ranking administrator positioned me to make a difference in other matters that had remained dormant or ignored. For instance, the Latina/o faculty and staff alliance had been trying for decades to establish a university recognized Latina/o, Mexican-American Studies (LMAS) major. They had reportedly overcome obstacle after obstacle and one broken promise after another. I gained oversight of this program development and cleared the extensive bureaucracy to make it happen. For instance, since all knowledgeable Latina/o tenure-track faculty had full plates from their extensive teaching, research, and service responsibilities, I had to find someone else to write and submit the program description and then move it through channels to be accepted in the course catalog. Upon obtaining the support of her department chair, I persuaded a non-tenure-track lecturer, whom I knew was interested in administrative experience, to complete the project. I obtained a minimum amount of money and, later, a course release to compensate her for the efforts. I also obtained support of the appropriate dean's office to make a space for the program in the college curriculum, and to strongly encourage their advisors to inform students about the benefits of the new program.

Today, the LMAS program offers a certificate, has numerous students, a proposal for an official major that is headed to the Board of Regents, its own physical space, a full professor at the helm, modest yearly funding for activities—and it is still growing. While I feel uncomfortable taking credit for making the program happen, decades of trying to get it done had proven fruitless until my presence and leadership changed the context. It took emotional energy to bring the program to fruition. I had to justify the value and necessity of the program to leaders with color-blind lenses. I met with and appeased multiple faculty and staff who wanted to know, "when are you going to create an Asian Studies, Pakistani Studies," and similar programs. As they accused me of caring only about Latinas/os, I patiently I explained that I would work to develop these other programs as soon as we had a critical mass of students who demanded them.

Of course, I cared about all faculty, but knew from experience that those who are tokenized in the university need more support than what is generally available in their departments. To be courageous, one must also be aware and unselfish. That form of valor played out when I opened up my home, my personal space, to bring together and create community for people who are traditionally marginalized. The gatherings were highly successful, filling my home and garden; they became a model for future social gatherings for different groups.

As I expected, there was resistance, e.g., "*Why didn't you invite us?*" "*Are you prejudiced against white men?*" Some administrators criticized me for not showing equal interest in gathering *all* faculty at my home. I knew this criticism was coming, but did it anyway, because it was necessary to provide support for those marginalized faculty to survive and thrive in the academy, and to eventually end the tokenism in academia. The chastising responses can feel like a no-win situation. People of color expect your support. Women of all races expect your support for "*women's*" (non-intersectional) issues. White colleagues expect you to be color-blind. I navigated that double bind with the confidence that my path was making a substantive difference for all persons, and eventually, for the institution, as I note later in this paper.

Speaking Truth to Power When the Powerful Is Your Boss

Fighting for equal treatment and representation of people of color has been a consistent theme in all my professional roles, with a range of heartbreaking and supportive personal and professional outcomes. In one position, the highest-ranked person in the room whom I'll call "Guy," who was one of my up-line supervisors, began viciously attacking a faculty diversity committee that was presenting a case for adding faculty of color across fields, and women in the sciences. Guy's attacks on the faculty became personal, even including cursing. No one was speaking up in defense of the committee. My mind was racing as to how to best intervene—to protect them, allow Guy to save face, and, possibly, to protect myself. Finally, I knew there was no way to do the latter if I spoke up. I'm not proud to say that it took me about twenty minutes of Guy's vitriol to gain the courage to speak up. I did so by praising the faculty, while not attacking Guy.

Nevertheless, the next day, Guy removed me from my administrative position and returned me to the faculty, in spite of the stellar performance reviews that I had received just recently. I felt pain and frustration because of the personal financial hit and the impact on my family, and because I was punished for doing the right thing. But I had no regrets about speaking up. The personal attacks on the less powerful were deplorable. The gratitude those faculty members expressed to me in private helped. As word of what happened spread across campus, a women's studies program was developed and funded, thus allowing university leaders to say they supported diversity. Most importantly, I preserved my personal, political, and professional integrity, which is central to my mental and physical well-being.

I had to decide whether to remain in the faculty or take on a different administrative role at another university. Was I willing to take another hit, if need be? By that point, I had enough experience to know that it would just be a matter of time before my bravery cost me my position. It was a difficult decision, but the calling of administrative service to make a difference for equity and for the marginalized people in the academy drew me back in.

I decided to accept a position at another university, moving my husband, who was supportive, but, frankly, he was well situated where we were. In my next position, along with doing the demanding job of the high rank, I continued advocating for fair treatment and representation, and speaking truth to power. And I continued looking for opportunities to affect change. For instance, upon hearing women faculty complain about sexist treatment, I repeatedly brought up these inequality concerns with various persons of power above and below the administrative hierarchy of my position, but they resisted the message. The lack of power to affect change in this matter was eating away at me. With the data spot-checking I conducted, I was certain that the perceptions of unequal treatment and expectations were not just figments of imagination, or "*over-active feminism*," as one male colleague called the complaints.

Then, all hell broke loose when the president's office released a holiday video that many women complained was sexist. I saw an opening to collect the needed data. I persuaded the provost and president to allow me to commission a special report to obtain data to determine, finally, whether there was any quantifiable evidence of gender- and race-based inequality on campus. I then cleared the bureaucratic landmines for the committee to obtain all requested data. The resulting report documented inequities in salary, workload, retention, and recruitment. It became a clarion call for change. Within three years, the administration provided funds to reduce faculty salary inequities. The work addressing other areas of inequity is ongoing.

For me, the most difficult and painful part of administration was the betrayal of colleagues. For instance, while I served in one of administrative roles, the university hired consultants to develop a comprehensive recruitment plan with a focus on maximizing our limited scholarship funds and human resources. The president asked them to focus on three university priorities: quality, quantity, and diversity. The consultants delivered the following audaciously racist salvo: "You can have quantity and quality, but not diversity; You can have quantity and diversity, but not quality. If you insist on diversity, you cannot have quality."

I felt disbelief that simmered into rage. Then, as I looked around the room for the reaction of the other high-ranking persons in the university, I was struck by their silence and calm demeanor. Their faces looked as though the consultants had just observed the obvious sentiment that education is important. The visible exception was the only other person of color in the room—a Latina woman who served as the Vice President for Diversity—whose face expressed disgust. The feeling of betrayal slowly consumed me. I had to speak up. But, I thought, *how do I speak up in a way that will not be interpreted as going against the president's hand-selected consultants?* Several seconds passed, though it felt like an eternity. While the consultants continued their spiel, I interrupted them to say that I was offended by their racist conclusion, for which they had provided no support except for biased stereotypes. The VP for Diversity and one of the white women agreed.

Every person in that room, in small group meetings and/or one-on-one, had expressed to me their beliefs about and commitment to changing the priorities and values that led to predominantly white university environments. So, how should I interpret their unexpected silence in this situation? At first, I surmised they were playing politics to protect themselves by not going against the status quo or against the consultants. Then, it dawned on me that they had been playing politics *with me* when they expressed values that they knew *I* would appreciate. After all, I was a strong, outspoken Senior Vice Provost for Academic Affairs—a more powerful position than those of most people in the room. My disdain for their politics further strengthened my resolve. I was using my energy to affect change, not play games just to keep my position.

I vowed to more consistently continue my gutsy acts of going against the mainstream. You see, I have not always spoken up, thinking that I must "pick my battles." However, since different people may be present at various times when racist, sexist, homophobic, or classist statements are made, it's important that all these persons understand that at least some of their colleagues consider their biases to be unacceptable and unprofessional in the workplace. I persevered because, otherwise, those who are busy playing politics and/or see nothing wrong with conclusions—like "you can't have diversity *and* quality"—will rule without resistance.

My bravery was not always punished. I received unexpected support when I was an American Council on Education (ACE) Fellow, which is a very prestigious and coveted recognition. At the time, the ACE method of teaching about diversity was to have the few Fellows of Color share intimate and painful memories of the various ways we had been injured by racism. The white Fellows were supposed to learn from our pain. It felt as though the Director, a white woman, was turning our misery into an ill-conceived talk show. I earnestly protested, although I was aware that the Director had the authority to remove me from the Fellows program on the spot. I suggested that, instead, perhaps white Fellows could share times in which they had been the perpetrators of racism, and what they learned from their actions. But she pushed back—so, I pushed back harder. I successfully persuaded my peers of color not to engage in this pageant of victimization. Upon returning from the ACE workshop to the host campus, I informed the president, my ACE supervisor, about what had happened, not knowing whether the Director had already contacted him. I braced myself to be told that I should have gone by the Director's rules and that he wanted me off the campus and out of the ACE Fellows program. Instead, this white male president of one of the largest and most prestigious research universities in the US looked me in the eyes and said, "I'm proud of you." He elaborated that it is rare to work with people who stand up for what they believe in, and that academia needed more leaders like me. I learned from a member of the next year's ACE Fellows cohort that the previous decades-long practice of victimizing Fellows of Color had ceased, and that my intercession had become legend, giving some other Fellows the courage to voice concerns.

Conclusion

Lest the reader believe that the only work I did as an administrator was to advocate for faculty of color, let me clarify. My various administrative roles involved vision, a 24/7 work ethic, and my successes have been numerous and significant to entire universities. These included balancing a college budget amidst a severe national fiscal crisis, developing and implementing policies and processes that significantly increased student retention, addressing salary concerns of advisors (most of whom were white), leading the revision of academic affairs policies to better protect all faculty, and obtaining over 40 million dollars in federal grants on which I was the Principal Investigator. In addition to my assigned work portfolio, I mindfully and consistently advocated for equity, especially for the traditionally underserved and marginalized. I did this work knowing that, in spite of my exceptional accomplishments, the stereotypic exaggeration and distortion of my efforts to increase equity is all that many people would notice or remember, especially because I worked in tokenized contexts that made me highly visible. As such, my time in each position was limited, so I had to make the most of it.

Today, I have once again been pushed out of administration. A new university president asked me to step back into the faculty. In many ways, I became the scapegoat for the changes that I led, which were good for the university, but were resented by persons who did not appreciate that a Mexican-American woman had such power and authority, especially when she used it to help traditionally marginalized persons. I do not regret the transition back to the faculty, especially since I knew the change was inevitable. I am proud of having had the courage to affect change that, even in a limited period, makes a difference—for individuals, for the collective, and in the institutional structure. Yet, I do not consciously think of myself as courageous. Rather, I strive to do the right thing by my personal, political, and professional values and identities. Today, from the rank of full professor,

I continue to challenge the disingenuous, neoliberal, color-blind perspectives that permeate academia. Most importantly, I mentor other people who will follow me in these perilous administrative positions; they will need guidance, and courage. Toward that end, I offer the following lessons that I learned in my tenure as a critically thinking and brave university administrator.

Precepts for Leading as Race-Conscious Women of Color in Predominantly White Institutions

1. Every action, word, meeting, and decision is political; some of your administrative colleagues are quite skilled at the politics and play constantly.
2. You must find communal support, and, as much as possible, be around people who love you for who you are and who share your values.
3. The higher the position, the more your employers will expect you to protect and promote the university brand in the manner respected by the status quo.
4. People of color will expect you to be their advocate in every way possible, while white colleagues want you to be "color-blind" in all your actions and strategic plans.
5. Sometimes the opportunity to affect change comes from unanticipated circumstances.
6. Since you will see the best and worst of the university, maintaining your integrity in your position is the ultimate challenge.
7. All of your actions and words will be very visible, but what will be most noticed and talked about are your efforts to improve the quality of life for people of color.
8. You serve at the will of your supervisor, so try to find cultural contexts and a vision that is consistent with your values.
9. In practice, change agents don't last in their position, so live within the economic means of your faculty fallback position, if possible.
10. The right person in the right place can make a difference. Therefore, we must have a seat at the table to affect change. Knowing we are making a difference with integrity is a reward that money cannot buy.

References

Niemann, Y. F. (1999). The making of a token: A case study of stereotype threat and racism in academe. *Frontiers: A Journal of Women Studies*, 20(1), 111–135.
Niemann, Y. F. (2003). The psychology of tokenism: Psychosocial reality of faculty of color. In G. Bernal, J. E. Trimble, A. K. Burlew, & F. T. Leong (Eds.), *The handbook of racial and ethnic minority psychology* (pp. 110–118). Thousand Oaks, CA: Sage Publications.

Niemann, Y. F. (2012). Presumed incompetent: Lessons learned from the experiences of race, class, sexuality, gender, and their intersections in the academic world. In G. Gutiérrez y Muhs, Y. F. Niemann, C. González, & A. Harris (Eds.), *Presumed incompetent: The intersections of race and class for women in academia* (pp. 446–499). Boulder, CO: University Press of Colorado and Utah State University Press.

Niemann, Y. F. (2016). The social ecology of tokenism in higher education institutions. *Peace Review: A Journal of Social Justice, 28*(4), 451–458.

3 What Looks Like Bravery in the Academy

Reflections of an African-American Woman Engineer

Gilda A. Barabino

In light of palpable marginalization and tokenizing in academia, just show-ing up on any given day constitutes a form of bravery for women of color aca-demics. In my own field of engineering, navigating a white male-dominated culture while carrying a knapsack of disadvantages based on the double binds of race and gender requires a special level of fortitude. In a climate where speaking out and challenging inequities prior to tenure is taboo, I was forced to break the rules in order to survive and thrive. Beyond my own professional success and well-being, I developed programs and initiatives to enhance the career success of people of color and women. I spoke out, even to the detriment of my own career and research, for the sake of others and in pursuit of improving the academy. While advocating for myself and oth-ers, I constantly remained aware that drawing attention to diversity would jeopardize my status as a respected researcher, and my career in general.

My journey has often been an isolating one, a path I deliberately chose in my refusal to remain silent in the face of injustice. In this essay, I reflect on the courage required to accomplish a number of career firsts in a profes-sional journey spanning over thirty years, and how these lived experiences have shaped my life's work in seeking equity and social justice in the acad-emy. Through these reflections, I hope to offer advice from one woman of color academic to another on being brave in our pursuits of personal success and equity for all in academia.

Bravery in the Face of Being First

Being "the first" is fraught with challenges and requires unwavering cour-age to meet those challenges, to break barriers, and to persist. I was the first African-American admitted to the graduate program in chemical engi-neering at Rice University in 1981, only fifteen years after Rice changed its charter to admit people of color. My unique status and the associated chal-lenges were heightened by my gender, training at a historically Black institu-tion, and by having a bachelor's degree in chemistry, rather than chemical engineering. I faced numerous obstacles, including carrying the daily weight of representing my race and gender, having my abilities questioned, and defying stereotypes and long-held beliefs on what a chemical engineering graduate student looked like. I persisted, obtaining my doctorate in 1986. Fueling my persistence was my determination to fight back, and my desire to hold the door open for those who would follow behind me.

Graduate school was not the last time I broke barriers and persisted in the face of bias and discrimination. When I became an assistant professor in chemical engineering at Northeastern University in 1989, I was the first African-American hired in the department and, at the time, the only assistant professor in the department. My fellow faculty members were senior white men, the majority of whom were approaching retirement. My unique status set the stage for professional challenges in the department.

A subset of my colleagues—all senior white men—formed the tenure and promotion committee, which was responsible for annual reviews of my progress toward tenure. At the crucial third-year review, the committee recommended that my employment be continued; however, their criticism was heavy and, in my view, unfounded. Their primary criticism was that I had not been sufficiently productive as evidenced by my failure to produce two publications per year since my arrival. It was inconceivable that I would receive such criticism when it took nearly two years for me to even have an operational laboratory, and I did not have the benefit of the standard reduced teaching load or graduate student support typically afforded to newly hired assistant professors. The review committee was blind to how I was severely and disproportionately overloaded in all aspects of research, teaching, and service and, further, to how my race and gender were exploited by having me provide representational diversity on nearly all departmental committees.

I knew that I had to respond to these criticisms in order to defend myself against an all-white male group of senior faculty who would be the ones voting on my tenure case a couple of years later. I decided to respond with a rebuttal letter. In the letter, I contextualized my experience to date to illustrate the lack of institutional support, the heavy teaching and service loads, the unrealistic expectations, and the total disconnect between the necessary support and the metrics for success. I made clear that blaming me as an individual faculty member for departmental and institutional inadequacies was unacceptable. I knew that I risked upsetting colleagues who held my professional future in their hands. My rationale was that if I should be afraid of their holding an accurate rebuttal against me, then I should really be afraid of being denied tenure based on a mischaracterization of accomplishments and being blamed for circumstances outside of my control.

I printed six copies of my rebuttal letter and placed one in each of my colleagues' department mailboxes. Then, I went to my office and sat at my desk nervously awaiting an inevitable call from the department chair, who always arrived early and checked his mail on the way to his office. As expected, he summoned me to his office to discuss the letter. He expressed how happy he was that he had caught me in time before the others had arrived to the office, and suggested that I remove the letters from their mailboxes to save myself from the wrath he feared was coming. According to him, I should be cautious about upsetting the people who would eventually vote on my tenure case; further, he suggested that it was not in my best interest to make them and department look bad to the rest of the university. I refused, leaving the letters for them to read. And, to be sure that they understood my rebuttal, I individually confronted each member of the departmental tenure and promotion committee to set the record straight and to provide my insight on how to more effectively develop a junior faculty member.

I realized that as a result of my actions, I could have been out of job and forced out of the academy with no guarantee of reentry. I realized that I was setting up a dynamic that could put me at further odds with my colleagues over the course of my time in the department. And I realized that I was in an environment that was never meant for me as an African-American woman. My deep personal convictions regarding equity and my refusal to stay silent and participate in my own oppression were what gave me the courage to stand up against their unfair evaluation. While the type of wrath and backlash that I was expecting did not materialize and I was told that, indeed, the department was rooting for my success, I remained on my own to achieve it. Ultimately, I was awarded tenure backed by a unanimous vote from my department.

In my post-tenure track life, I found that breaking barriers as "the first" was no easier and required no less courage than it had in graduate school and while on the tenure-track. I learned this upon accepting a position as the inaugural vice provost for academic diversity (VPAD) at Georgia Tech. The VPAD post was created to guide the institution's strategic development efforts to increase diversity in research, education, and service. After a protracted national search that proved to be unsuccessful, the decision was made to fill the position internally, ideally hiring an individual with a proven record in research, education, and diversity. I considered applying for the position, though I understood the inherent challenges, the career risks (e.g., diversity work dismissed as a dead-end or career-killer), the enormity of the work, and the threats of the unknown. I heard the concern and warnings voiced by colleagues, administrators, friends, and even foes. I also recognized that the most pronounced and inherent danger to my career was the backlash associated with becoming a highly visible diversity champion in a formal role. Being perceived by colleagues as a diversity champion rather than as a researcher or scholar has very negative career implications at any and all points along the career path, especially for a woman of color and especially in a technical field like engineering. Yet, consistent with my convictions to pursue equity and justice, I accepted the position of VPAD while simultaneously holding the position of associate chair for graduate studies in my department.

My role as the first VPAD, in addition to my being the only vice provost and the only woman of color serving on the President's Cabinet, placed me in a precarious position. I was often the only voice to speak out on thorny issues associated with inequities based on race, ethnicity, and gender. In one salient example regarding a faculty retention initiative, I was the sole voice in the President's Cabinet to point out the imbalance between women and men in the initiative, and that women are less likely than men to be vocal or forceful about seeking outside opportunities. More broadly, the issue at hand was a culture that tended to be less supportive of the career advancement of women and an obvious need for sustained effort to affect a shift in that culture.

The bravery required in carrying out the role of VPAD is best reflected in day-to-day experiences, and less so in major, one-time acts in extremely risk-filled environments. Most impactfully, I led by example in showing up, assuming risks, and speaking truth to power on behalf of diversity. I beat the drum and stood my ground when there was the inevitable pushback and resistance to the message and to suggestions for new approaches. I assumed these risks as VPAD because of a sense of responsibility for paving the way for others. I often feared that failing to do my job would provide confirmatory evidence for those who believed that African-Americans were less capable, reducing the chances of another African-American academic following in my footsteps. I felt the weight of representing my race and gender, and the associated baggage of stereotypes and lowered expectations for African-American women in particular. It was also of paramount importance to me that others did not have to go through what I went through.

As the first and only African-American woman in many of my professional roles, I have been a magnet for faculty, students, and staff of color who looked to me as a role model, a survivor, and sometimes as a savior to help them get through the rocky path I had already traveled. I do not take these responsibilities lightly. For example, during my second sabbatical as the only African-American woman engineering professor in the Institute for Bioengineering and Biosciences, students lined up at my office door on almost a daily basis. So much so that I started hosting group meetings over meals to better manage my time and reach the ever-expanding group seeking my support. In these meetings, I assigned readings from the social sciences and advocated self-empowerment. I began collaborating with psychology professor Kareen Malone to hold focus groups. We used the common threads that emerged from shared experiences as the basis for our published study on identity formation for women of color scientists and as the foundation for these meetings. This work was an impetus for the research-driven professional development initiatives I established to support women of color faculty.

How I Have Persisted

Women of color are faced with racial and gender inequities that, when left unaddressed, threaten our career progression, health, and well-being. It is critical that we adopt strategies to socialize women of color into the academy and enact policies and practices to ensure supportive environments where women of color can thrive. In my own work and that of others (Turner, 2002; Henderson, Hunter, & Hildreth, 2010; Leggon & Barabino, 2015), I have found that professional development, networking, and mentoring are effective mechanisms for professional socialization towards career advancement. I have also found that understanding what feeds our souls helps to foster courage and support advancement.

For example, over the years, I have come to appreciate the power of the mind and having an appropriate mindset. Through my ascension from engineering faculty member to dual roles as researcher and university administrator, fear of taking on too much or facing a stereotypical threat simply because I was a woman of color never deterred me. I have been careful to compartmentalize behaviors, both mine and those of others, in an attempt to distinguish between what is under my control and what is part of social and institutional factors that adversely impact all women of color academics. Rather than let my anger at persistent inequities consume or derail me, I seek to channel my energy toward efforts for positive change that will make the academy a more welcoming place for all of its constituents. I choose to be driven by inner strength and self-empowerment to avoid being overcome by a defeatist attitude. This attitude brings to mind lyrics sung by Patti Labelle, "I'm feelin' good from my head to my shoes—Know where I'm goin' and I know what to do—I tidied up my point of view—I got a new attitude."

Beyond this attitude, I've learned to adopt a warrior mindset when the situation demands it. Dealing with the continual aggressions—both micro and macro—that women of color are confronted with carrying out their responsibilities in academia requires the fortitude of a warrior. When I know a hostile environment or situation may be awaiting me on the other side of the door, I approach carefully and with the mental armor of a warrior, prepared to do battle if necessary. I am in great company in this approach. Black feminist Audre Lorde, a self-proclaimed warrior and prolific writer on racial and gender discrimination, took on the name Gamba Adisa (warrior: she who makes her meaning known) in an African naming ceremony in her later years. We can learn a great deal from Lorde in her writings and how she lived her life. She wrote, "When I dare to be powerful, to use my strength in the service of my vision, then it becomes less and less important whether I am afraid" (p. 13). Indeed, when we, as women of color, empower ourselves, when we break the silence, come to voice and speak truth to power, when we stand up for justice, when we arm ourselves with mental armor, and when we overcome adversity through the actions of our empowered selves, it is less important whether we are afraid.

My trailblazing experiences have reinforced my confidence in my own talents and decision-making. I, like many women—women of color, in particular—became accustomed to dipping into unchartered waters without the benefit of role models and mentors; accustomed to stepping out on my own navigating what often turned out to be treacherous paths; and, accustomed to resistance and other forms of adversity. Among the things that have helped me be resilient and given me staying power was a recognition early on that staying silent on the sidelines was not an option, that I was my own best advocate, and that, ultimately, I was responsible for choosing the path that I would follow and where it would take me.

Crossing disciplines and looking to the social sciences to better understand social and organizational dynamics in the academy was a tactic I adopted early on as an assistant professor. My goal was to use what I learned as a means of survival: to help me and others better navigate the academy, to avoid perils, to become socialized in the profession, and to thrive. To address the unique challenges facing women of color, I established the Cross Disciplinary Initiative for Minority Women Faculty through a National Science Foundation (NSF) ADVANCE grant and asked sociologist, Cheryl Leggon, to direct it with me. I led and continue to lead the NSF-funded Minority Faculty Development Workshop established in 2001 and the National Institute for Faculty Equity founded in 2010. These initiatives are all in keeping with my philosophy of standing up for myself and for others, and maintaining a sense of self-empowerment for the greater good.

My parting advice to other women, especially women of color, is simple: don't be afraid! It's advice that I have followed in my own career and is based on a lifetime of fearlessness.

Specifically, don't be afraid to:

- Be yourself: You cannot be successful trying to be someone you are not. It is important for us to know and be our authentic selves and to own and cherish all of our identities.
- Speak out: There is nothing to be gained by remaining silent when the context demands that your voice be heard. Break the conspiracy of silence and speak out.
- Take risks: Context matters and there is little in life that does not come without risks. Measured risk-taking can make the difference between advancement and regression and it has the potential for measurable and immeasurable rewards.
- Take a stand: What do you stand for? Be true to your values and convictions.
- Champion diversity: Diversity and excellence are inextricably linked and are the true drivers of advancement.
- Chart your own course: You are your own best advocate and best positioned to know what is right for you. While charting your course, also define your own metrics of success and career milestones.
- Arm yourself: Arm yourself with knowledge and mental armor (the appropriate mindset) to ensure success. The power of knowledge and the mind cannot be overstated.
- Fail: Fear of failure can be crippling and can impede growth, development, and success.

Most importantly, don't be afraid to be fearless. Be brave!

24   *Gilda A. Barabino*

References

Henderson, T. L., Hunter, A. G., & Hildreth, G. J. (2010). Outsiders within the academy: Strategies for resistance and mentoring African American women. *Michigan Family Review*, *14*(1).

Leggon, C. B., & Barabino, G. A. (2015). Socializing African American female engineers into academic careers. In J. B. Slaughter, Y. Tao, & W. Pearson, Jr. (Eds.), *Changing the face of engineering: The African American experience* (pp. 241–255). Baltimore, MD: JHU Press.

Lorde, A. (1997). *The cancer journal:*(Special Edition). San Francisco, CA: Aunt Lute Books.

Turner, C. S. V. (2002). Women of color in academe: Living with multiple marginality. *Journal of Higher Education*, *73*(1), 74–93.

4 Being Brave in the Ivory Towers as "Zape-tah-hol-ah" (Sticks with Bow)

Robin "Zape-tah-hol-ah" Starr Minthorn

Introduction

Hatso (greetings in Kiowa). My name is Robin "Zape-tah-hol-ah" Minthorn. Zape-tah-hol-ah is my Kiowa name given to me by my maternal grandma; it means "Sticks with Bow." It was her mother's Kiowa name, and I am honored to carry it with me. I grew up in Oklahoma but remain connected to my family in Oregon. I am Kiowa, Apache, Nez Perce, Umatilla, and Assiniboine. I am also a proud granddaughter, daughter, sister, partner, auntie, and mother. I introduce myself in this way—saying my "Indian" or "Kiowa" name and how I am connected to that tribal community—because it is consistent with Indigenous community practice. This tradition, however, is an act of resistance within the academy, where most scholars hardly acknowledge their own cultural traditions. Rather, academics typically acknowledge their academic title and affiliation first.

While negotiating academic spaces, it is important for us as Indigenous women to continue to honor the roles we have in our families and communities.[1] We[2] must have both of our feet planted in the academy and the community as Indigenous scholars. For this reason, being brave is reflecting and acting on what it means to be a Kiowa woman scholar and, in turn, what that means for me to remember my ancestors, the students who are watching me, and the community with which I should work and impact. Though we are regularly pressured to leave out who we are or put our identities last in order to conform to the expectations of the academy or institution, I constantly reflect on my Indigenous identity and embody the values and memory of my ancestors. This commitment often comes into conflict with norms of the academy and, at times, comes at the expense of being seen as a known scholar and gaining more notoriety for the promotion and tenure process. Relationships with others, especially with those within the Native American community, come before the tenure process; in addition, perpetual learning should be at the heart of our efforts to negotiate space in the academy and the communities that surround our institutions.

In this essay, I share my journey in the academy as an Indigenous woman warrior scholar. I honor my Kiowa, Apache, Nez Perce, Umatilla, and

Assiniboine roots and ancestors daily through my actions, publications, and heart work.[3] This means honoring who I am in my culture and identity, which inform and guide my work, while also using any influence I have to advocate on behalf of, and do work that creates space for, others. In creating this space and honoring who I am, I am attempting to Indigenize the academy.

Bravery in Action

Honoring My Community

My work to Indigenize the academy is partly driven by my efforts to honor my tribal community and other Indigenous communities in New Mexico, my family, and my home community. This work is crucial because all institutions of higher education sit on Indigenous land (Lipe, 2012). Indeed, it should be a common practice to acknowledge Indigenous peoples and to include the voices and perspectives of members of the Indigenous communities that surround the college or university in our professional work.

An example of my efforts to Indigenize the academy is my work to create the Native American Leadership in Education (NALE) doctoral cohort. Such work is pivotal to Indigenizing the academy because the program was designed to respond to community needs, centering the Indigenous perspective and experience during its creation rather than as an add-on. Though I was hired as a tenure-track professor at the University of New Mexico (UNM) because my research focuses on Indigenous leadership, I did not assert myself as an expert. Instead, I insisted that the doctoral cohort for Native American students in educational leadership be accountable to the community and their needs and what they wanted, not what I thought as an academic.

The process of developing the program, including creating curricula, approaches, and support structures, took two years and twenty meetings. I used an intentional approach, rather than rushing to create the program to meet some existing need in the institution; rather, I took the time to include community perspectives. My team and I surveyed forty tribal leaders in New Mexico and Indigenous educators in K-12 and tribal college settings to identify the strengths of the communities and to determine what the curriculum and programmatic outcomes should be. We also solicited feedback from tribal communities in New Mexico and Indigenous education sites throughout the program's development. We created a NALE advisory board that represents some of these communities to provide updates on the cohort and to receive feedback on the process of the cohort itself. From creation to implementation, I prioritized community voices at every step of the way in the NALE doctoral program.

Though meaningful, this work was hard to do as a tenure-track professor because junior scholars are pressured to focus primarily on their research.

Just as we are discouraged from doing service, we are not encouraged to put importance on honoring the community's voice. I sometimes wondered what senior scholars and administrators would think of my advocating for the process of including the community's voice. Would I be reprimanded or lose credibility as an scholar? Would my professional relationships or annual evaluations suffer? Would my strong commitment to honor my own identity, values, and community hurt my chances for tenure and promotion? Indeed, I was aware that initiating a process that honors Indigenous voices as a tenure-track professor was risky.

I was able to minimize these potential risks by finding allies. I found support from the faculty in the Educational Leadership (ED LEAD) program. In addition, I had three different College of Education Deans who agreed that we should include voices from the tribal nations and Indigenous communities in developing the NALE program. I provided regular updates on the progress of receiving community feedback to the faculty and deans. I coordinated meetings with the community to maintain their support and input. And I did all of this while remaining productive in my scholarship.

In fall 2016, my ED LEAD program colleagues and I started the first NALE doctoral cohort with seven Native American doctoral students. The orientation and induction process for the NALE doctoral process defies tradition. Many academic programs start their doctoral students into their program through formalized orientations that go over program requirements, processes to know, and other academically oriented topic areas. The NALE doctoral cohort orientation does much more, including starting their process off with a prayer in an Indigenous language and gaining an understanding of how they see Indigenous leadership and education. The new doctoral students are invited to write down their motivation for completing the doctoral degree, specifically in the NALE program. Later, I encourage them to reread this note during the hard times in the doctoral process to help them persist.

Another aspect of the induction process was that each of the doctoral students brought their families to campus to acknowledge their role in the doctoral journey and to be a part of their induction into the program. The family members varied from grandmothers, mothers, fathers, aunties, uncles, brothers, sisters, partners, children, grandchildren, and others. Each student introduced their family and each student was gifted with cedar and other gifts to acknowledge the beginning of their journey. We now have a family gathering every semester to bring all of the families together to be a continuous part of the doctoral process and to celebrate accomplishments. The NALE doctoral cohort is now a recognized doctoral cohort locally and nationally.

Standing with My Community

Another way I work to Indigenize the academy is by supporting Indigenous student-activists on campus. I often stand with these students as they push for greater inclusion of Indigenous voices and resist practices that exclude Indigenous perspectives. One example of standing with student-activists is through my support for the UNM Kiva Club. The Kiva Club is one of the oldest Native American student organizations in the country; it is well known for its social activism on campus and in the community. As their advisor (beginning spring 2014) at UNM, I have used my own networks and voice to advocate on their behalf.

For example, in fall 2014, the Kiva Club began efforts to remove recognition of Columbus Day from the UNM academic calendar and replace it with Indigenous Peoples Day of Resistance and Resilience. Columbus Day as a holiday honors Christopher Columbus, whose legacy includes murder, rape, genocide, and forced assimilation of Indigenous Peoples across the Americas. Renaming this day to honor the Indigenous Peoples is one small step in righting the wrongs of honoring settler colonialism and patriarchy on college campuses. In their effort to rename the holiday, the Kiva Club held meetings with other various student organizations, including other Native student groups, as well as Native students not tied to organizations on campus, to propose a resolution to the undergraduate governing group. Their goal was to reach a consensus on the wording of the proposed resolution. They successfully proposed the resolution, which the governing body passed; however, it then remained stalled.

I sat with Kiva Club in these meetings, offering suggestions as needed, but mostly being a constant source of support by being present. Although I served as their faculty advisor, I was still conscious of my own status as a junior faculty member. I knew there were potential risks in supporting activism aimed at challenging the university, especially as I sat in meetings that administrators, faculty, and community members also attended. But I remained steadfast in my support of the students and their efforts. Because of the various relationships cultivated and work I had already done for campus diversity initiatives and local Indigenous communities, I could provide an extra layer of advocacy during committee meetings with faculty and administrators. To date, the removal of Columbus Day and replacement with Indigenous Peoples Day of Resistance and Resilience continues to be stalled as upper administrators advocate for what they see as a more acceptable and broader naming for the proposed Indigenous Peoples Day.

During the 2015–2016 academic year, the Kiva Club expanded its efforts to Indigenize UNM by abolishing the racist UNM presidential seal. The seal includes a conquistador and frontiersmen, who represent the colonial history of the state of New Mexico. This problematic seal minimizes Indigenous peoples and other peoples in New Mexico who have helped make the university and state what it is today. Working with a community group called Red Nation, the Kiva Club launched a movement to abolish the racist seal, including a campus protest during Nizhoni days in April 2016. During this protest, I chose to speak out as an Assistant Professor, Kiva Club's faculty advisor, and as a recent board member for the National Indian Education

Association. Toward the end of this protest, the students delivered a letter with a list of eleven demands addressed to the university president. I walked into the president's office with them and stood with them as the encounter was livestreamed on social media. In our recorded confrontation with him, we captured his condescending and defensive reaction to our presence and purpose while he accepted the letter and list of demands.

Afterwards, we walked back to the protest site outside of an administrative building, where the student protestors began burning images of the presidential seal. I was handed a copy of the seal and briefly contemplated whether I should join this revolutionary act. I decided to burn the seal, while momentarily wondering how this action might impact my tenure and promotion or presence on campus. But the concern about repercussions was fleeting. I acknowledged that being their advisor meant standing with them on social issues, not only because they think they are important, but because I think these issues are important, too, and most importantly, the community does. Fortunately, I did not face any backlash, though these actions were photographed and my statement at the protest was placed (with my permission) on the Red Nation's website. Native student leaders and others remarked that they appreciated my presence to help give them strength as they held this protest. The solidarity and support I offered meant more than any repercussions or reprimands that I might face for my involvement.

The Kiva Club's campaign to abolish the racist presidential seal continued in the spring. I have supported them at each step, advocating for them in various venues and meetings with any influence or say I might have through my own involvement on campus. For example, as they attended campus fora hosted by the Diversity Equity and Inclusion Office, I attended to support their efforts to educate others about the history of the seal, why it was racist, and why it needed to be abolished. I coordinated meetings with upper administration on behalf of the Kiva Club and attended UNM Board of Regents committee meetings and general meetings about the seal. Though I have contemplated what others might think of my actions and the potential negative impact on my career, standing with the Kiva Club and the broader Indigenous community at UNM has meant much more to me than the risks or reprimands that might be a result of the efforts to Indigenize UNM. Fortunately, I have not faced any backlash; rather, by lending my support as a faculty member, I have influenced others around campus and in the community to stand with the students as allies.

Empowering My Community

The final way in which I work to Indigenize academia is by using my research to create space for other Indigenous scholars. In particular, I pursue scholarship and scholarly practices that honor who we are in our culture and ways of thinking and being. As an Indigenous scholar, I not only have chosen to honor my voice in my writing style, but also choose to deviate from standards that do not honor this voice. I have chosen to engage in collaborative work that is necessary and that I feel should be accepted in the promotion and tenure process, regardless of discipline. In addition, I resist American Psychological Association (APA) standards for writing that conflict with Indigenous voice and contributions.

These practices are reflected in a book I co-edited, *The Indigenous Leadership in Higher Education*. This book is the first of its kind to discuss Indigenous leadership in higher education. My co-editor and I included narratives from Indigenous student leaders; we felt that it was essential to do so as we often talk about and research students in higher education, but do not ask them to contribute to our work. Perhaps our most important contribution was to set a precedent for Indigenous scholars to cite the deviation from APA standards in writing by using "we" instead of "I." APA format encourages staying consistent in person and tense, but Indigenous scholars often alternate between "we" and "I" and use variations of time (i.e., past to present, present to past, etc.). In addition, though the APA style guide suggests italicizing words in foreign languages, we did not italicize text written in Indigenous languages. Indigenous languages are not to be considered foreign languages, as Indigenous peoples are the original peoples. We also capitalized "Indigenous" and "Elder" throughout our book because of the revered status that Elders carry in our tribal communities. Instead of conforming to APA standards, we chose to go against the grain to broaden the use of Indigenous voice and perspectives that can now be cited in hopes of helping to empower current and future Indigenous scholars to honor their voice in writing.

I did worry somewhat about receiving judgment within our discipline and failing to find a publisher willing to publish the book and, consequently, how this might affect my tenure and promotion and my scholarly productivity. But the benefits outweighed the risks to me. These acts are much more important than any repercussions or pushback that might be received in higher education. Pushing against the norms in an academic press can result in helping others honor their voice and presence in the academy if we (I) just keep standing up for our voice and standards in writing.

In a second, forthcoming co-edited book, *Reclaiming Indigenous Research in Higher Education*, my co-editor and I seek to provide space to assert the use of Indigenous methodologies that deviate from the standards often set in higher education scholarship. We invited recent doctoral graduates, junior faculty, and one tenured faculty member to share how they Indigenize their research through their own perspectives, knowledge, and/or the use of Indigenous methodologies. This edited volume provides higher education faculty, scholars, and graduate students with recommendations for how to acknowledge our scholarship and to support Indigenous graduate students in higher education. We resist the empirical status quo by placing the Indigenous perspective first in the format of the chapters and the approach in the conclusion that honored collaboration instead. This could have received resistance by the university press but they chose to honor our purpose and approach to the book. We each have a responsibility, with any influence or ability we have, to empower other current and upcoming Indigenous scholars in our work.

Conclusion: "Success" and Honoring Yourself

In sharing these examples of my efforts to Indigenize the academy, I hope that others are inspired to be true to who they are as Indigenous women scholars and in whatever other roles they might have, not only at home and in the community, but also in the roles they gain as they move through the academy. When we start our journey in academia, we must remind ourselves how we got there, who supported us, and whom we represent. Doing so is inherently brave because many academics fail to reflect on their own identity and honor those individuals who are a part of their journey.

Pursuing an academic career can be a very egotistical and individualistic process that can engulf and discourage this reflective process. One act that has helped me remain true to who I am while on the tenure-track is consistently reminding myself of the values that are most important to me in my scholarship and teaching: collaboration, community, and respect. When we remind ourselves of who we are, we are more likely to be genuine and to honor ourselves, our communities, and our families. I recommend that we always remain true to ourselves and our values. That is what "success" should look like for us all of us.

As brave women scholars of color, we should stand beside our students of color in their movements on campus and in their communities. We should also be making room for emerging women of color and, in my case, Indigenous women scholars who, I believe, will have fewer obstacles to overcome because of me and others who are pushing the envelope. We all must work together to reclaim our spaces and our rights while defining how education should be delivered to and by our (Indigenous) communities. There is a great deal of work that must be done in changing the norms of how our academic programs function, namely to ensure that the community's voice is included in informing our curriculum, approaches, and expected outcomes.

That is my purpose as Zape-tah-hol-ah. We (and I) are always representing our (my) ancestors and communities. I am an Indigenous woman warrior scholar who is constantly working towards honoring my community, standing with my community, and empowering my community. We are the answered prayers of our ancestors.

Notes

1 I must acknowledge the many Indigenous women scholars who have paved a way for me to be here and to share space with them. I am one Indigenous woman scholar sharing my story; I know there are many similar stories and others whose bravery is not shared. It is with this acknowledgment that I share my story and

hope others know they are not alone on this journey through the ivory towers that were not made for us.

2 I choose to utilize "we" and "I" interchangeably. Not that I speak for anyone but when I speak as an Indigenous scholar, I represent my community and the sentiments of other Indigenous women scholars whom I work alongside and with.

3 Heart work is the work that we, Indigenous scholars, do on behalf and with our communities not expecting or wanting any payback or rewards. It is selfless and passionate to help benefit those whom we hold close to our hearts.

References

Lipe, K. (2012). Kēia ʻāina: The center of our work. In J. Osorio (Ed.), *I ulu i ka ʻāina: Land* (pp. 99–109). Honolulu, HI: University of Hawaii Press.

5 "Working the Cracks" in Academia and Beyond

Cultivating "Race" and Social Justice Convergence Spaces, Networks, and Liberation Capital for Social Transformation in the Neoliberal University

Nancy López

Introduction

"*¡No dejes que nadie te robe tu derecho!* Don't let anyone ever rob you of your rights!" my mother would always say whenever any of her five children faced injustice. My passion and ethical commitment to resist oppression *all of the time* is not a choice; it is a matter of survival that was instilled in me at a very young age by my mother. My modus operandi is to speak truth to power, act, and reflect in order to advance systems-level transformations. I know no other way.

I am an AfroLatina, a hypervisible, racially stigmatized woman. I am the eldest of five US-born children of Dominican immigrants. My parents never had the privilege of going to school beyond the second grade. I grew up in public housing projects in New York City and, in 1987, I graduated from a *de facto* segregated large public vocational high school for girls in the city. I am also the first woman of the African Diaspora to earn tenure at the largest college of a large public university in the US Southwest. Against the backdrop of my immigrant mother's struggles as a single parent, I realized that any of the challenges that I faced in the ivory tower of academia paled in comparison to that of many brave Black women, like my mother. Contributing to liberatory praxis in the form of conversations, action, and reflection, is my small way of honoring the legacy of many brave women of color who fought to create a more just future for me, my daughters, and future generations to come.

In this essay, I reflect upon my work to create a Center on the Study of "Race" and Social Justice at Southwest Public University (SPU).[1] No matter where we find ourselves, we can all engage in what Collins (2000) refers to as "working the cracks"—advancing sustainable racial justice work from inside bureaucracies. It does not matter whether your sphere of influence is located within the neoliberal, color- and power-evasive university, or within or with community-based organizations, government agencies, nonprofits organizations, or even the private sector (Bonilla-Silva, 2017). Racial justice and other emancipatory projects should be assessed only in terms of the substance and impact of the work—not whether one is credentialed (Collins, 2000). I end the essay with a discussion of concrete strategies for advancing racial justice transformations within and beyond academia. It is my hope that everyone engages in crafting their own racial truth-telling narratives and concrete strategies for advancing racial justice and equity within their spheres of influence.

Creating the Center for the Study of "Race" and Social Justice

For years, I spoke about the need for an interdisciplinary convergence space at my university for race and social justice scholars who critically engaged normative approaches to race. While on the tenure-track, I found that some colleagues were hostile to my critical work on race and racialization, including one-third who voted against my tenure case because my work made them uncomfortable (Zambrana 2018). Indeed, even in my experience of teaching and presenting at a variety of public and private universities throughout the country, I received ongoing messages that speak to the risks of engaging in racial justice scholarly production and praxis: "Your work is just based on your experience, so it is not scholarly." "Intersectionality is garbage." "There is no such thing as white privilege." "Racialization is jargon." "Your talk about race and racialization makes us uncomfortable." Regardless of the intentions behind this feedback, comments that disparage your scholarship and praxis send a loud and clear message to students, faculty, and others who engage in racial justice work in the academy: your ideas, thoughts, scholarship and praxis are not welcome, are deficient, or do not "fit." Given my strong record, I eventually earned tenure, but I felt compelled to challenge the racist status quo that frequently penalizes scholars of color for doing critical race scholarship.

When Dr. Laura Gómez joined SPU, we felt a natural affinity for each other as scholars and as people in general, particularly as the only two Latina tenured sociologists on campus. At our many lunches, coffee dates, and playdates with our children at a local children's science center, we puzzled over why SPU was touted as a Hispanic-Serving Institution (HSI) and also boasted having one of the highest critical mass of Native American students in the country, yet did not have an interdisciplinary research center dedicated to race and social justice. We approached a variety of administrators who politely endorsed the idea of such a center, but always responded that there was no funding available to start one. Besides funding concerns, we knew that there were other risks to starting the center. Conventional department annual review guidelines do not value and sometimes even actively discourage these efforts as "service work" that supposedly hamper one's promotion to full professor. Disrupting the racial status quo of implicit and explicit oppressive ontologies and knowledge projects could be seen as an attack on mainstream scholarship. We decided the potential professional costs were worth the risk of establishing an interdisciplinary center on race and social justice scholarship, teaching, and community engagement.

Eventually, a funding opportunity arose that we immediately pursued. In 2007, a major private foundation awarded SPU multi-million-dollar funding to establish an interdisciplinary unit focused on health policy. The key mission of the unit was to cultivate the next generation of scholars from underrepresented racial and ethnic communities that would become leaders in health policy to improve the health of Native American, Latinx, and other marginalized communities. We saw this as an opportunity for leveraging the center and we seized it.

While getting coffee on campus in Fall 2008, I bumped into the executive director of the newly established center on health policy. I immediately pitched our idea, sharing the vision and mission for our proposed center. I explained that a Center for the Study of "Race" & Social Justice would function as an interdisciplinary hub for scholars, students, and community leaders who critically interrogate normative approaches to race scholarship for social justice and policy ends. I noted that we intentionally placed the word "race" in quotation marks in the title of the Center to trouble common sense understandings of race as biology or genes or culture and instead shift attention to how race is a social construction that is most visible when we interrogate racialized power, privilege, ideologies, and processes at the structural, institutional, and interpersonal levels. Through our work, we sought to highlight how race and racism as social constructions have real consequences for health, wealth, education, employment, housing, and other measurable outcomes. After a series of conversations and submitting a concise proposal for the Center, we successfully convinced the executive director to grant us two years of seed money for programming activities; by January 2009, the Center for the Study of "Race" and Social Justice was born!

One of the first activities of the Center was a year-long lecture series, "Troubling 'Race': Cutting Edge Approaches Across the Disciplines." This created a convergence space for researchers from physical anthropology, fine arts, health sciences, social sciences, and law, as well as students, staff, and community members to come together to interrogate normative approaches to the study of race across the disciplines. Because of the relevance to the community, these lectures attracted many local scholar-activists who worked with and through nonprofits and other organizations to support the community.

Simultaneously, we launched a faculty and graduate student study group, inviting scholars from law, health science, social sciences, and humanities. By utilizing interdisciplinary readings that focused on the limitations about how "race" was being conceptualized in our respective disciplines, we aimed to create a community of practice among scholars who did work on inequalities broadly but were interested in learning more specifically about race and social justice. The following year we created a transdisciplinary "race" working group that focused on producing guidelines for researching "race" based on our collective interdisciplinary insights. Perhaps our most tangible deliverable was our National Institutes of Health (NIH) R21 funded 2010 workshop that materialized in our 2013 co-edited book, *Mapping "Race": Critical Approaches to Health Disparities Research*.

Leveraging Interest Convergence

To keep the Center afloat, continue programming, and expand our efforts to advance racial justice on campus and in the community, we have often had to work to leverage our goals with those of the university. Despite the early success of the Center, I faced a dilemma by the third year: Dr. Laura Gómez left SPU, accepting a position at another institution. Additionally, the two-year seed funding from the health policy research center had run out. Despite these realities, I refused to give up and let the Center experience a natural decline. I leveraged my networks and sought ad hoc internal funding at SPU through partnerships with other established centers, institutes, programs, and departments that have dedicated operating funds and staff and also focus on issues of social justice and equity. This support often came in the form of in-kind support via work-study students who worked on specific projects. With the new sources of funding, I was able to convene an interdisciplinary symposium on the politics of racial and ethnic measurements for the 2020 Census. The symposium included the former director of the US Census Bureau and staff at the Office of Management and Budget (OMB), as well as diverse scholars from multiple disciplines. The symposium received support from high-level faculty administrators who were eager to leverage the publicity that would come from this event.

Since the 2011 symposium on the future of Hispanic origin and race data collection, I have been actively engaged in national debates around the 2020 Census. Through engaging in conversations with diverse academic, policy, and practitioner communities, I developed a measure of race/racialization I call "street race"—that is, what race you think other people in the US automatically assume you are based on what you look like (López, Vargas, Juarez, Cacari-Stone, & Bettez, 2017). This conceptualization highlights how the color line maps onto inequalities among Latinx communities (López, 2018, 2017). Most importantly, by underscoring the idea that race/racialization has a visual component, whereby one's appearance is used as a master social status that has implications for how one is treated by others—particularly those in positions of power—the "street race" concept has the potential to dislodge genetic and biological ontologies of race (Omi & Winant, 2015).

We unsuccessfully attempted to secure additional funding from other foundations, national funding agencies, and other potential supporters. But, even without sustainable funding, the work of the Center continued.

It was at this time that we established an Advisory Board for the Center, comprised of faculty from across the social sciences, education, and health sciences at SPU. These faculty embody interdisciplinary expertise that spans the breadth of fields, as well as the diversity we seek to advance in terms of inclusive excellence. Our lack of funding made it impossible to continue to invite speakers from around the country to give talks as part of the lecture series on "troubling race." But we were able to draw from expertise and passion from around our own campus to continue the Center's work.

We decided to leverage our only sphere of influence that cannot be taken away from faculty as a matter of academic freedom: curriculum. In 2015, we submitted a proposal to create a 15-credit, transcripted race and social justice interdisciplinary graduate certificate—the first in the country. We knew that this was a rather bold move because the Center had a liminal status, lacking official recognition as an academic program with a designated course code for classes. So, we attempted to convince the university of the feasibility of the proposed certificate by compiling a laundry list of existing courses from every college, department, and discipline and win buy-in from upper administration.

Among the first questions that administrators asked were the usual ones: "How much will this cost? How will this help students get jobs?" We understood the relevance of critical race theory's *interest convergence principle*—the idea that small progress in racial justice is possible when it speaks to the interests of those in power. As such, we appropriated the language of the neoliberal university by emphasizing that this certificate would make SPU stand out as a "destination university," attracting scholars, students, and staff from across the country and the globe (Bell, 1980). We did our best to sell the idea that approving the certificate was in the financial interest of the university. Further, we provided the university with a list of hundreds of jobs in race and social justice, arguing that this transcripted certificate would give our students a competitive edge.

We succeeded in getting the certificate on the books in less than a year and the university appeared to celebrate it in a news story dedicated to this accomplishment. Although seemingly small, this victory has had ripple effects as many other programs have begun to have conversations on race and social justice in the core curriculum and they continue to send us syllabi for consideration for the list of approved courses for the certificate. We successfully avoided backlash to the certificate's creation by cultivating buy-in from multiple colleges, disciplines, and departments, and including over seventy classes that already existed in the course catalog, as we continually work on improvements.

Bouncing Back from Failure

Doing liberatory work within the neoliberal university will, inevitably, come with failure. But resilience and perseverance are crucial to moving ahead. In

Fall 2016, emboldened by the embrace of the graduate certificate, the Center Advisory Board quickly learned the limits of interest convergence. We proposed the creation of an undergraduate version of the graduate certificate but were unsuccessful. The reasons given by university administrators were, again, part and parcel of the discourses circulating in the neoliberal university: "We value the spirit of the work, but given our ongoing budgets and hiring freeze we cannot overburden existing staff with additional advising for a new certificate program at the undergraduate level."

To no avail, we presented evidence showing that these types of classes and programs enhance student success and would improve six-year undergraduate graduation rates. To counter arguments of the lack of staffing for the certificate, we identified staff who expressed an interest in this work. Although, in the end, these compelling arguments did not change the immediate decision to reject the proposed undergraduate version of the certificate, members of our Advisory Board met with administrators. They agreed to write a letter of support affirming the value-added by an undergraduate certificate. And, perhaps most importantly, they agreed to help us identify creative ways of supporting the establishment of the undergraduate version of the certificate during the hiring freeze with the understanding that we would resubmit the proposals in the future.

We also submitted syllabi for two new "RACE" catalog courses: 1) "Race & Social Justice: Interdisciplinary Insights" and 2) "Race, Rights and Reparations," which is currently being taught by a colleague through other funding. We also developed another class on "Race and Pedagogy: Interdisciplinary Praxis." However, the response of the white high-level administrators operating from neoliberal university logics was swift and unrelenting: "When we approved the Race and Social Justice Interdisciplinary Graduate Certificate last year, you said you would not create new courses!" To which the advisory board, affiliated faculty, and other students affiliated with the Center replied: "By supporting the undergraduate certificate, SPU has the opportunity to lead in national innovations in interdisciplinary race and social justice scholarship, teaching and community engagement." High-level faculty administrators would not budge, even as we explained that we receive frequent queries from other universities across the country asking how they can replicate what we are doing.

We refused to give up. Immediately after seeing each of our innovations deflated and rejected, we scheduled a meeting with key administrators and posed the following question: "Are there any initiatives to advance interdisciplinary innovations?" Despite the temporary brakes on our efforts to create innovations in race and social justice courses, we successfully carved out a space for conversations among administrators to talk about the need to account for nimble institutional structures that cultivate interdisciplinary innovations. In the meantime, we were already at work on Plan B. We compiled a list of faculty members who received support from their chairs for offering the proposed courses as cross-listed courses and posted the interdisciplinary syllabi as a resource for others on the Center website. We continue to build the infrastructure and political will for these courses and are confident that they will be approved in the future. In the meantime, we have posted our co-created syllabi, proposal, and materials so that anyone can access the fruits of our labor. We continue to receive inquiries from all over the US requesting advice on how to launch similar classes, certificates, and centers, which affirms the importance and impact of our work in spite of roadblocks.

Another silver lining and a glimmer of hope emerged. At our Fall 2016 graduate student potluck, approximately thirty students and faculty were in attendance from just about every college and academic program in the university. Several in attendance were recent graduates who heard about the certificate and felt compelled to attend. Because of their feedback, we were able to submit another request to create two pathways for completing the certificate: one for current students, and one for those who already possess an undergraduate degree. We were able to secure institutional support for this; the proposal was approved in Spring 2018. To be sure, in our first-year of existence, we have a working list of fifty to sixty students who have expressed interest in the certificate, have officially enrolled ten students, and celebrated our first graduate!

Cultivating Liberation Capital for Transformation and Social Justice in Academia

If you are interested in resisting the neoliberal university, it is imperative that you realize that, even if there is little, if any, support for race and social justice work, we can all do something. As documented by Morris (2015 p. 188), we need to create "liberation capital," just as W.E.B. DuBois did with his network of insurgent scholars, both inside and outside the university. By engaging in what Collins (1998) refers to as "speaking our truth" and "working the cracks" or using our insider knowledge of how the system works to advance social justice, we can make a difference, even when we are not funded. Toward that end, I provide three suggestions below.

First, cultivate your race and social justice *familia* because it takes a village. Find networks of resistance wherever you are. Networks matter, vision matters, politics matter, logistics matter, and impactful and transformative deliverables matter. Always remember that you are part of a larger *familia* in the struggle for liberation and that everyone has something to contribute to these efforts no matter where you may find yourself.

Second, leverage self-reflexivity to plant the seeds of consciousness for potentially liberatory social transformations. I often begin discussions with administrators or other audiences with an invitation to self-reflexivity about their positionality. I ask: "What's Your Race-Gender-Class-Sexual Orientation Social Location & Experience? Consider how this shapes your understandings about inequality and social justice" (López, Erwin, Binder, &

Chavez, 2017). By setting the stage for everyone to listen, think about their own lived social locations in intersecting systems of power, privilege, and oppression, we can set the stage for advancing empathy and hopefully praxis (ongoing critical listening, reflection and action anchored in justice and equity) (Collins & Bilge, 2016; Collins, 1998). As Collins (1998, p. 24) explains:

> When feelings are involved—when individuals *feel* as opposed to *think* they are committed—and when those feelings are infused with self-reflexive truths as well as some sort of moral authorize, actions become fully politicized.

In my case, self-reflexivity involves acknowledging that despite the multiple intersecting systems of oppression I faced—including race-gender profiling, growing up in concentrated poverty, and attending *de facto* segregated under-resourced schools—I also experienced the unearned invisible privilege of birthright citizenship and the spoils of heterosexism—privileges that many of my own relatives, friends, students, and other community members growing up in the same neighborhood and attending the same schools, could not count on (Johnson, Rivera, & López, 2017; López & Gadsden, 2017).

And, finally, never forget that academic freedom is our right, no matter our academic rank or student status. When colleagues admonish me that "all your talk about race and racialization is making others uncomfortable," I respond that I, along with others in academia, have the right to do research, publish, teach, and engage in service that engages racial justice work. While in many departments, colleges, and universities, critical scholarship on race and other intersecting systems of power may be disparaged as "political" and "ideological" (as if all scholarship weren't inherently ideological and political) or criticized for not meeting "the bar," we can invoke the notion of peer-review and academic freedom as cornerstones of the academic enterprise.

The next time that colleagues admonish you to choose between conventional mainstream scholarship or public scholarship, remind them that this is a false choice. You can do both. Always contextualize your work as "Engaged Scholarship and Teaching" in your tenure and promotion documents. Just document how this scholarship is being co-produced with community partners and how it is being disseminated and impacting policy and practice beyond academia. You also can provide a list of peer-reviewers who are qualified to assess the value and impact of your work for scholarship; you can also list those who are not qualified to do so. Several disciplines including sociology have developed guidelines for evaluating public scholarship, so one small action item would be to have these guidelines officially recognized in the tenure and promotion guidelines in your department, college, and university faculty handbook. Again, it is your right!

Revolutionary liberatory transformations will not happen overnight, and these efforts will most likely not be funded in the neoliberal corporate university (DeLeon, Katira, López, & Valenzuela, 2017). However, all hope is not lost. As one of my sisters in the struggle, another Black woman colleague and mentor, told me: "If we wait for the funding to do our work, we will never get anything done." We must engage in liberatory struggles for transformation on a daily basis no matter whether we have funding power. We will always have people power.

Remember that any form of resistance, no matter how small, can plant the seeds for sustainable liberatory transformations as part of a never-ending struggle to advance a more perfect union for all. Hopefully, in the years ahead, you can collaborate with passionate scholars, community members, and students who are committed to questioning the racial status quo in order to create advances, no matter how seemingly small, that contribute to sustainable transformational liberatory change.

Note

1 "Southwest Public University" (SPU) and "Center for the Study of 'Race' & Social Justice" are pseudonyms. I use the word "race" in quotation marks to underscore that race is not a genetic or biological reality; rather, it is a socially constructed relationship of power and social status that is visible at multiple levels of power, including the individual, institutional, and structural levels of analysis.

References

Bell, D. A. (1980). Brown v. Board of Education and the interest-convergence dilemma. *Harvard Law Review*, *93*(3), 518–533.

Bonilla-Silva, E. (2017). *Racism without racists: Color-blind racism and the persistence of racial inequality in America*. Lanham, MD: Rowman & Littlefield.

Collins, P. H. (1998). *Black women and the search for justice*. Minneapolis, MN: University of Minnesota Press.

Collins, P. H. (2000). *Black feminist thought: Knowledge, consciousness, and the politics of empowerment*. New York, NY: Routledge.

Collins, P. H., & Bilge, S. (2016). *Intersectionality*. Malden, MA: Polity Press.

DeLeon, J., Katira, K., López, N., & Valenzuela, N. A. (2017). Navigating resistance to antiracist and anti-oppressive curriculum in a diverse public university: Critical race theory, the fetish of 'good intentions' and social justice praxis. *International Journal of Curriculum and Social Justice*, *1*(2), 11–68.

Johnson, R. G., Rivera, M., & López, N. (2017). Social movements and the need for a trans ethics approach to LGBTQ homeless youth. *Public Integrity* 19: 1–14.

López, N. (2017). Why the 2020 census should keep longstanding separate questions about Hispanic origin and race. *Scholars Strategy Network*. Retrieved from www.scholarsstrategynetwork.org/brief/why-2020-census-should-keep-longstanding-separate-questions-about-hispanic-origin-and-race

López, N. (2018, February 28). The US census Bureau keeps confusing race and ethnicity. *The Conversation*. Retrieved from https://theconversation.com/the-us-census-bureau-keeps-confusing-race-and-ethnicity-89649López, N., Erwin, C.,

Binder, M., & Chavez, M. (2017). Making the invisible visible: Advancing quantitative methods through critical race theory and intersectionality for revealing complex race-gender-class inequalities in higher education, 1980–2015. *Race, Ethnicity and Education*, 21(2), 180–207.

López, N., & Gadsden, V. L. (2017). Health inequities, social determinants, and intersectionality. In K. Bogard, V. M., Murry, & C. Alexander (Eds.), *Perspectives on health equity and social determinants of health* (pp. 3–24). Washington, DC: National Academy of Medicine.

López, N., Vargas, E., Juarez, M., Cacari-Stone, L., & Bettez, S. (2017). What's your "street race"? Leveraging multidimensional measures of race and intersectionality for examining physical and mental health status among Latinxs. *Sociology of Race and Ethnicity*, 4(1), 49–66.

Morris, A. (2015). *The scholar denied: W.E.B. DuBois and the birth of modern sociology*. Berkeley, CA: University of California Press.

Omi, M., & Winant, H. (2015). *Racial formation in the United States*. New York, NY: Routledge.

Zambrana, Ruth. 2018. Toxic Ivory Towers: The Consequences of Work Stress on Underrepresented Minority Faculty. New Brunswick, NJ: Rutgers University Press.

6 Resisting Sexual Harassment in Academia

Tayler J. Mathews

I was inspired to write this essay because I understand it as a unique moment to bear witness. My objective is to highlight the reality that many women of color scholars encounter in our efforts to pursue advanced degrees, as I rarely see my reflection in the stories concerning sexual and gender-based violence in academia. While I am moved by *any* woman who has faced this injustice, I cannot help but feel a bit distressed. I cannot help but ask, *if this were a Black woman, would anyone even care? How many Black women are experiencing this in silence? Where are they, and what might they need to hear?* Thus, I have chosen to share pieces of my own narrative, as a Black woman who has experienced sexual harassment and sexist discrimination, while offering direction to embolden other women of color students in our fight for a fair education that is free from these forms of violence.

My struggle for gender equity in academia is as much concerned with affirming my Black womanhood inside my community as it is with fighting against external sources of oppression. I am honored to be a graduate student at a historically Black university. Yet, while my campus community shares a rich history in the struggle against racial injustice, the civil rights that prescribe equity in the interest of gender have yet to be fully realized. No matter the racial and ethnic particularities of your institution, sexual harassment and other forms of gender discrimination are likely to materialize. Violence of this kind is ubiquitous, and, as a woman of color, addressing it is especially risky. Sexual harassment can have detrimental consequences for one's ability to access education. Declining someone's unwanted advances—particularly if they occupy or are connected to those in a position of power—can initiate retaliatory actions that serve to compound the harassment. Indeed, this has been my reality throughout my PhD experience. In a patriarchal culture that regards women as readily available and blames us for the violent acts committed against us, while protecting and infantilizing perpetrators, it can feel as though there are few ways to obtain recourse when we are violated.

Despite an ever-increasing list of colleges currently under federal investigations for Title IX violations, many students who encounter harm because of their gender never report experiencing sexual violence. This decision is further complicated by one's racial and ethnic identity. Reporting perpetrators of the same background may engender pressure to stay silent as a display of community solidarity; for Black women, challenging sexual violence perpetrated by Black men may be seen as "airing dirty laundry," or even feeding into racist stereotypes about Black men's sexualities. But I refused to remain silent. By sharing my personal story, it is my hope to empower others to report and seek justice for any form of gendered violence they may be facing. I understand the hostile and intimidating environment that you are confronting while trying to work towards your academic objectives. You may be unsure of how to move forward, and perhaps you feel too psychologically exhausted to continue. I am all too aware of how institutions can make us feel isolated in our struggle. Yet we can still resist, as we hold within us the power of bravery.

Reporting and Backlash

When I began my first semester of my political science doctoral program, I also began experiencing sexual harassment. It was particularly difficult to fathom, as I had yet to acquire the language and framework that I needed to understand what was happening. Though I was familiar with the term *sexual harassment*, I doubted my intuition. I did not want to magnify the situation or be labeled as a paranoid woman who was deceitful. I worried that I would be blamed for attracting the unwanted attention, and that no one else would consider this mistreatment as seriously harmful. These concerns were not foolish; indeed, many of these worries materialized after I decided to formally report the harassment. Although I was unaware of the magnitude of the decision at the time, this would serve as my first act of bravery.

When I initially reported my concerns to faculty and staff members, I did not say, "I am being sexually harassed." Rather, I described the many troubling incidents and expressed my increasing uneasiness about the situation. I was unaware at the time that these employees were legally obligated to take my complaint to the university's Title IX coordinator, and to inform me of my rights under the university's sexual misconduct policy in compliance with Title IX—a federal civil right. I would later discover that the university did not even have a Title IX coordinator.

The faculty weakly attempted to assure me that I need not worry about being harmed. Nevertheless, the harassment did not stop. In fact, it continued well into the next academic year. It was not until I began researching sexual harassment in the workplace and in public spaces (i.e., street harassment) that my own circumstances were furthered illuminated. The stories of the women whom I studied were *my* story. They had a right to seek justice, and so did I.

However, I encountered difficulty locating my university's Title IX resources. I was fortunate to have a friend who knew more about Title IX than I did. With their help and encouragement, I completed a written statement detailing the harassment. As a further matter, I included the failure of faculty members to fulfill their obligations as "responsible employees," and the general absence of university-wide Title IX resources. This report served as a significant juncture in my PhD experience. Not only was the investigative process deficient—by which I mean that there was no thorough investigation of my reports—my case was also closed without any notification to me. Moreover, faculty refused to recognize my federal right to an accommodation, and trivialized the terror that I felt at even the thought of having to continue to share classroom space with the harasser. As I continued to encounter obstacles accessing a fair and safe education—free of discrimination *and* retaliation—I also continued to learn more about Title IX policies. The more I learned about my rights, the more empowered I became. I knew I had something on which to stand—federal law. Because I refused to accept the assaults on my rights, I faced aggressive reprisals from university faculty and administrators.

I also became increasingly cognizant that I was one of many students facing gender discrimination and retaliation. Several students believed that they could not risk challenging the university and, under the hostile circumstances of my experience, I understood their apprehension. Yet, I recognized that I was already a target and I could not turn away from the abuses that I encountered or observed. I voiced my concerns both in person and in writing. I went to administrators' offices, I made phone calls, and I furthered my research. I was and continue to be determined to create something better because students deserve better. Perhaps this can be identified as righteous anger—an emotion that has motivated me to push for change. I was aware that my experience of sexual harassment and gender discrimination was not unique. There are far too many people navigating the daily assaults against their identity, bodily integrity, and intellectual capabilities. I knew that if I did not speak up it was likely that few others would either. I could not live with knowing that I did not at least challenge the predatory and hostile environment, especially in light of the reality that women would still meet this abuse even after I advance from the university. Something had to change. The truth needed to be told. Eventually, I decided to file a complaint with the US Department of Education. Thereafter, I secured legal counsel from a local non-profit organization.

In what follows I present several of the lessons that I have learned throughout my journey. I have included guidance that may prove useful to you whether you are contemplating how to move forward or you have already initiated the reporting process at your institution. Remember, you are not alone in your struggle.

Struggling Against Injustice

When struggling against gender injustice in academia, it is essential that you be informed about your rights under Title IX law. Title IX of the US

Education Amendments of 1972 is a Federal Civil Right. This law prohibits gender-based discrimination, which includes sexual harassment, in educational settings. Websites such as Know Your IX (knowyourix.org) and
End Rape On Campus (endrapeoncampus.org) are immensely informative
resources that I regularly consult. While universities are required to implement their own policies in accordance with Title IX, this information may
be difficult to locate or comprehend. In spite of this, it is imperative that
you know your institution's policies and procedures, or at least what little
information is available to you. For instance, I examined numerous student
and faculty handbooks, and inspected the university's website. I knew which
policies existed, I knew which policies were absent, and I knew which policies contradicted other university policies (and, in some cases, federal law).
This gave me an advantage in my numerous communications with faculty
and administrators who were not informed of, or perhaps simply did not
care about, their responsibilities. My awareness of Title IX equipped me
with an armor of confidence, fortifying my commitment to proceed.

You should absolutely ensure that you are aware of your institution's policies and procedures (or lack thereof), while simultaneously utilizing external
resources that explain your rights and options. Indeed, knowledge is power.
It is important to familiarize yourself with the behaviors and definitions
that constitute the various prohibited forms of discrimination under Title
IX, and *document everything* along the way. After you have exhausted your
university's reporting channels, you have the right to move forward and utilize external options. You may even find yourself with enough to evidence to
request investigations from your institution's accreditation organization and
the US Department of Education (e.g., Office of Inspector General, Office
for Civil Rights, and Family Policy Compliance Office). Again, you have the
right to report discrimination to your university and to expect timely and
corrective action. Should the redress of abuses fail to transpire, you have a
right to advance to agencies outside of your institution, without guilt.

Although you may feel afraid because of the circumstances you are
encountering, I am convinced that fear does not have to immobilize you.
Fear is normal; given the challenges you are confronting, it is likely that
you will have moments of hesitation. The truth is that your fear will accompany you whether you decide to take action or not. One of the reasons why
I remain motivated to push through my own angst is that I find inaction
much more daunting than any sense of fear. Inaction produces no results,
no answers, and no direction.

Like me, you may worry that speaking out will jeopardize your opportunity to obtain your degree. However, you must keep in mind that surrender-
ing to your circumstances is not an assured path that will guarantee that you
meet your objectives. By denying your own reality you are still taking a risk;
you are still compromising your mental and physical health, your safety,
your grades, your career, and your future. The risk is the very same, if not
greater. What additionally pushed me to move beyond my fear is knowing

that I could not live the rest of my life as a feminist advocating for survivors while neglecting my *own* rights. If for no one else, this is something that I had to do for myself because I am worth fighting for. You, too, are worth fighting for. You must give yourself the same support and commitment as you give to other causes. After all, when you fight for your right to have an education that is free of gender discrimination and sexual violence, you are fighting for others, too.

To all women, I recommend: speak up. Speak *loudly*. Speak *firmly*. Speak *with conviction*. When you choose to struggle against injustice, you can acknowledge your fear again and again, and you can continue to move forward.

As you struggle on, you will likely receive a great deal of advice. While some words will be kindhearted and affirming, there is another category of advice of which you should be aware. This particular form of guidance, usually delivered by well-intentioned sources, is notably deceptive: *put your head down, get your PhD, and get out*. This was, and still is, perplexing. And, to be perfectly candid, this is not good advice. Perhaps I draw this conclusion because I do not consider acquiring a PhD as the ultimate goal. *A goal*, certainly. Yet not an endeavor that requires me to deny my humanity. I reject any notion that suggests the negation of my womanhood—putting myself on hold until I cross over as an official member of the academy.

Fighting for justice is not something you do *one day*—it is something you do *every day*. It is something you do now. Besides, there is no guarantee that you will be successful *with* a degree (whatever "success" is anyway). You do not put your humanity on hold until after you have acquired some credentials. There are no "PhD" stipulations for your rights. Do not concede to anyone who discourages you from fighting for yourself. Live your truth, and as you clarify the direction of your path, you may find others walking on the side of justice along with you. They may even become your beloved comrades, sources of hope to ease feelings of self-doubt and isolation.

Still, I must be transparent about how painful this journey can be. I certainly do not believe that one is obligated to find "the good" in a horrific situation. Some of life's events are excruciating, they are disorienting, and they are traumatic in a way in which you will not be the same after you recover. Nevertheless, much of my ability to endure the anguish of my present circumstances is inspired by the revolutionary love that I have found among other student-activists. I invoke *revolutionary love* with sincerity. These students have affected my life in such a powerful and profound way and I have been transformed into a stronger person because of meeting them. Even on my worst days, knowing that I have these individuals in my corner has been enough to propel me to keep going. After the painful betrayal by what was once my cherished university, meeting these students rejuvenated and reconnected me to the roots of my campus community. You may also find this awe-inspiring support on your campus, in your city, or even on social media. No matter where you locate your comrades, or "movement fam,"

I strongly encourage you to join a movement and/or organization that is fighting for issues that are important to you. You may need to try on more than one organization to find the perfect fit, yet I can assure you that when you discover this kind of love, it will be absolutely transformative.

While love and support can nurture your strength, there is no getting around the fact that you will become a target when you challenge the status quo. You may lose opportunities, you may be demonized, and your name may be abused and exploited. And still, you can *thrive*. I am firmly committed to being a voice of dissent in the face of wrongdoing. This is an element of myself that I embrace, even though many do not welcome my voice or my persistence. My activism has been described by faculty as a refusal to "adjust" to the "leadership" of the institution. Certainly, I refuse to adjust to injustice. At one point, I even faced a disciplinary hearing, accused of "furnishing false information to the university." It was a brazen act of retaliation and still stands as an egregious violation of my rights. It was also an act of intimidation, a message that said, "speak up and we will come after you." Through the continued legal support of a local non-profit women's organization, I was ultimately found "not responsible" for this accusation.

My advice for confronting retaliation is straightforward: you must be prepared for the campaigns that will be launched against you. When you challenge patriarchal authority, you will face vigorous opposition, and although this can be painful, you can continue to resist. As you meet enmity and mendacity, be assured that it is still possible for you to flourish. You can move beyond these moments of vicious opposition.

When you fight against forces that are attempting to deny your experience of sexual and gender-based violence, and prevent you from receiving a fair education along with educational benefits, you will change. You will become stronger, though you may have moments when you feel powerless. You will know the inhumanity of individuals whom you see daily, persons on whom you once believed you could depend. You will move beyond your initial naiveté about institutional policies, enforcement, and administrative integrity. You will grow. By claiming your autonomy, you can decide how you will meet the various challenges you come up against.

What I knew with certitude was that I would not allow my experience to infix a hateful spirit and, most importantly, I refused to relinquish my joy. Of course, this has been an arduous undertaking. I am angry about what is happening to me, yet I have not allowed that emotion to consume me. I will always be angry about sexist discrimination. However, being angry *about actual injustices* does not negate my spirit of buoyancy. I do not believe that one has to eradicate their anger and feign forgiveness in order to move forward. I may be angry about this real, concrete violation for a very long time. Indeed, something abominable has happened to me, and I am still living through its effects.

At the same time, I have examined this experience in a way that has pushed me to reevaluate myself and the person I desire to become. I seek to develop myself in ways that ensure that I never fail anyone the way that I have been failed. The lessons of what not to be, of whom not to become, have not been missed. After my own exposure to a considerable degree of indifference, I am motivated to become more compassionate. I seek to live a life of authenticity and integrity instead of merely appropriating righteous rhetoric. On this journey of self-cultivation, rooted in the spirit of justice, I am willing to reflect and push myself to grow and improve.

I encourage you to identify your values and ask yourself: who do you want to be during and after this process? You are not responsible for the harassment perpetrated against you nor are you to blame for the misbehavior of those who are required to ensure your safety and well-being. You have a right to be infuriated, and you also have a right to joy and tenderness.

A Final Note on Bravery

I will always remember my PhD experience as a struggle for my humanity: the right to exist in an educational space without being subjected to sexual harassment, discrimination, reprisals, and cruelty. I will remember those who stood by my side, and I will remember the strangers who took me in and believed me without question. I will also remember those few faculty members and administrators whom I feel I cannot name without compromising their employment. Their continuous support serves as a courageous act against concerted efforts to obscure real truths. Some have commented on my own bravery, although I did not feel very brave when I reported sexual harassment. While I note the absence of conscious bravery, I most certainly am aware that my journey is no small feat. It takes courage to report any type of abuse once. It takes even more courage to continue reporting these incidents after it is conspicuously evident that the problem has not only been allowed to continue, but has additionally become intensified by vigorous attempts to keep you quiet. It takes courage to file a federal Title IX complaint with the US Department of Education's Office for Civil Rights, and it takes courage to continue to fight for the right to obtain a fair and safe education after your peers, professors, and administrators have made it clear that your very presence is a problem.

Still, much of my courage has come from certain naiveté. I actually believed that if I reported harassment, then my institution would do everything in their power to help. I was wrong. Nonetheless, I was not willing capitulate to the forces of patriarchal status quo. I found additional motivation to continue the fight after learning that several other women and queer students were also encountering gender discrimination.

My experience informs me that bravery is no mystery. Anyone can be brave. You need only make the decision to act. Bravery is a decision to move forward, regardless of difficulty, in the direction of truth and justice. Bravery is refusing to be intimidated by risk because you know that inaction is also a risk. Although you may remain silent in a moment of danger (because it is not always safe to directly confront perpetrators), you do not allow the incidences to *keep* you silent. You may choose to report at a later time, you may choose to join an organization that fights against injustice, you can advocate, you can teach, and you can write. These are all acts of bravery.

Acknowledgments

I express my deepest gratitude to my family for their unconditional love and encouragement. Thank you for giving me the space to always be myself. Thank you for making me brave.

I would also like to thank my second family, my comrades, my movement fam. Thank you for giving me a home in our campus community when I felt alone and abandoned. Thank you for your commitment to justice. Thank you for your friendship and for your love. Thank you for being unapologetically you: Jill Cartwright, Eva Dickerson, Da'Shaun Harrison, Venkayla Haynes, Clarissa Brooks, and Jabarey Wells.

7 Un-Disciplined

A Conversation Between Two Sisters Who Left Graduate School

Aph Ko and Syl Ko

Between December 2016 and February 2017, Aph and Syl Ko (sisters) held a series of conversations via Skype in which they reflected on their respective decisions to leave graduate school. In 2014, Aph rescinded an offer to attend a PhD program after obtaining her master's degree in communication. Syl resigned from her PhD program in philosophy during her fifth year in 2016. Following the tradition of other Black feminists who acknowledge the power of presenting issues of the day within the context of "kitchen table conversations," the Ko sisters have taken the relevant excerpts from these discussions (and left them in their original form) to highlight in what ways leaving academia constitutes an act of bravery, especially for Black women.

APH KO: Syl, you and I have been Skyping for a few weeks now, reflecting on the theme of bravery, but we're only now beginning to touch on how *leaving* graduate school might count as a really courageous act. (laughs)

SYL KO: Right! I think I was struggling with this because I definitely felt like a loser when I realized I couldn't go on. The other graduate students repeatedly told me how much courage it takes to just up and leave. But the looks on their faces and the tone of their voices suggested that they thought I was making a huge mistake. "You're only one year away from graduating! You would have definitely landed a job!" Every time they said that word, "courageous," I'd flinch because it was clear that they weren't using it in a positive way. So, when we started talking about this in the context of providing inspiration or even as activism, I felt that I might be the wrong person to talk to because I was still feeling ashamed for leaving. How is being a "quitter" an inspirational story, you know?

APH: Doesn't it remind you of military rhetoric? Our cohort is like a troop and we all have to make it to the end! We'll have some battle wounds and survive plenty of scars, but that just comes with the job! And, then you get to be a decorated citizen! Somewhere along the line, I snapped out of this dream of decorated citizenship and realized that I was in a waking nightmare. A majority of the graduate students were drinking every day and suffering from depression and anxiety. The only thing that anyone could afford on one's pittance of a stipend was coffee despite the enormous amount of labor put into teaching and research. And, this was all laughed off as "typical grad school life." I was sick all of the time. I had no social life whatsoever. My relationships were suffering. I was told that this was the price one pays for pursuing knowledge. But, I began to wonder whether these things really had anything to do with that.

SYL: Lots of studies suggest that minority graduate students are impacted even more negatively given that they tend to come from disadvantaged backgrounds and have to navigate microaggressions and so on. But, I remember that you were specifically concerned about something that tends to remain on the margins of these sorts of discussions surrounding race and higher education. You were concerned that minority students, especially Black students, were being *brainwashed* and that this was detrimental since these very people are those who will go on and serve as professors and leaders in Black communities. These will be the voices that *represent* "the Black experience."

APH: Right. "Brainwashing" tends to be understood in a superficial sense. That is, brainwashing is thought of as covertly smuggling certain explicit content. You know, something like teaching Black kids that they are inferior by constantly showcasing and underscoring the "achievements," lifestyles, belief systems, or whatever of white people. Or, only mentioning Black people in the context of slavery, social justice, or in "redemption" stories. But, I'm referring to something else in higher education. I'm talking about being brainwashed into disciplinary thinking. There is this really oppressive tendency to speak *through* our discipline, even when we're addressing something as basic and felt as exploitation. It's as if we've been conditioned to see things happening in the world and even to ourselves through the eyes of the purified, sterilized methodologies of our fields. If we can't present these harms or grievances in the form of a research project (one that would have the full support and backing of our adviser and chair, of course!) or in appropriate academic language, then we're scared to talk about them, scared to do something about them, or scared that they aren't important enough to waste energy on. Our minds are being shaped to fit the contours of the manufactured and seemingly arbitrary lines that are drawn in academia to separate fields from one another. This obscures which events or situations qualify as problems and even how we can act on them.

SYL: It sounds as though you are saying that it is like you woke up from the dream of "decorated citizenship" when you realized we are being *disciplined*. Disciplinary thinking is a way to keep us in line, to force us to conceive of the world and even our own problems in a certain way. When we deviate from this way of thinking, we are penalized by not being taken seriously, not being published, not receiving tenure . . . and then, of course, there's the social ostracism that will occur when you have to interact with your colleagues and others in your field.

APH: Exactly. On the one hand, of course, I understand the push for higher education, especially in our community. Historically, Black people have been denied access to (quality) classrooms, teachers, and resources, and this has affected what kind of lives we can have and the kinds of people we can be. On the other hand, we're handing our minds over to curricula, syllabi, and knowledge systems that have no interest in us as human beings and, in fact, that help to maintain the narrative that we are *not* human beings.

SYL: Yeah, and even more than that—there is a lot of emphasis on the *content* of what we're learning and teaching in schools. There's the whole "diversity" thing happening, wherein everyone is trying to pepper their syllabi with the right amount of minoritized or marginalized writers, thinkers, and so on. Honestly, I still don't quite get when "diversity" became a thing! But, anyway, there's been a general failure to investigate the walls separating one discipline or field from another—and the same with subfields—and how this plays into keeping things as they are. I came up against these disciplinary walls so many times when I was trying to plan out my dissertation research. I can appeal to *this* writer or tradition, but not *that* one because, technically, that one isn't "real" philosophy . . . it's "only" cultural studies or history or something like that. If you try to push against this, now you're infecting the methodology so *clearly* you don't quite "get" it yet!

APH: You just put into words what I was feeling during my MA training. (laughs) These constraints—and my constant inquiring into the nature of those constraints—started to hinder my work. I was having more and better ideas. I just wanted to focus on developing those. Lots of opportunities were presenting themselves to me because of the ideas about which I wrote. I realized that trying to accomplish these kinds of projects in academia was not going to happen. My projects were becoming more and more radical by mainstream academic standards. And, I began to see that a part of being radical is *resisting* disciplinary measures, understood in the colloquial sense, but also in the academic sense. So, I rescinded my acceptance to a PhD program. I was really scared to go out on my own without the structure or legitimacy of a sanctioned program. But, now, I have no regrets.

SYL: It seems being in school was really important for you, though in a different way than you anticipated. By experiencing the limits of disciplinary thinking—and how this is reflected also in the social world with its many compartments—you came to realize that many issues simply can't be addressed unless a new space is constructed. And that's precisely what you went on to do, Aph! You have your own organization, you're a mentor, important people turn to you for guidance and commentary, and you're always at a new place giving a talk and inspiring people.

School was a stepping stone, but away from itself. I'm always so proud of you, by the way.

APH: I couldn't have done it without you, Syl, and the rest of the family helping me along the way. You were so supportive! That feeling of being "a loser" that you mentioned earlier is something that I definitely experienced, too. Because the nature of my projects didn't fit in with the academic space I was in, I felt so lost. I fell into a deep depression and could barely function. But, once I left school, I felt even more lost for a while. I wasn't sure what I'd do with myself or how I'd afford to live as a writer. I asked myself, "what am I doing with my life?!" I think that, from the start, I went to school just because I was lost in general. School can temporarily give you a feeling of direction and so it can operate like a reprieve from the general anxiety of life. It's easy to be seduced into continuing on. But, once I finally felt as though I had a life project, I began to suffocate there. It was really helpful when you started telling me about the concept of "undisciplinary thinking," which is spreading in decolonial circles. It was the first time I stopped judging myself and embraced the implications of what I was doing.

SYL: Right, *un*disciplinary, as opposed to *inter*disciplinary work. I learned about that from a course I took with decolonial scholar Walter Mignolo. It blew my mind.

APH: It did a world of good for me to hear about that. There's so much interesting stuff going on, but when you're in school, you're locked into a rigid epistemic location. We can't see what everyone else is doing and we aren't allowed to let it affect us. Again, there are the lines drawn to keep the world the way it is and it prevents those of us who are minoritized from *really* talking to one another.

SYL: It takes a lot of courage to say that, Aph. I know that some of your closest friends take academic life seriously. They do not question how the institution of academia itself serves to protect the legacy that we are all trying our best to rid ourselves and the world of. There is this idea that being included is, in itself, an expression of dismantling the system, but being included doesn't necessarily precipitate dissolution. If anything, it might add an extra layer of protection to the legacy.

APH: Yeah, it took me a long time to see myself as brave. Again, Black folks have been fighting for a long time to have the right to education and to be included and represented in books and syllabi. I have lost a lot of friends and opportunities because of my critical stance toward academia. People who I hold in very high regard have come to see me as an enemy to diversity.

SYL: I suppose that's the price one pays for being a radical thinker, though. I think that you have to be very brave to follow through after that moment when you realize, first of all, this is not the way that you want to live. I know firsthand how difficult it is to have a certain career path that everyone respects but, because it is draining your soul, you refuse to do it anymore. But, I think it is even more difficult to accept that what you *thought* was something that would help your community (and yourself) might actually be a detriment to it, especially after you've invested so much time and energy into it. You had so many people who believed in you while you were in school and you probably would have had a great career. But, you left all of that behind because you believe that, not only is that stuff making us sick physically and psychologically, but it is also not going to liberate us.

APH: I'm glad you brought up the issue of liberation with respect to bravery because that seems to be the main motivation behind both of our decisions. Everyone is constantly talking about liberation, liberation, liberation on the grand scale . . . but we can't even liberate ourselves from this diseased and very peculiar notion of what education or knowledge is.

SYL: One might say, then, that liberation is actually scary terrain. It's generally not presented that way, though. Liberation will require "ending the world"—as some Afropessimists say—and reimagining or starting a new one—as some Afrofuturists say. It will take a lot of courage to bring about both of these phases. When you left school for the reasons you did, that is one part of the collective step to move past what we have and enter the future.

APH: It's funny, though, because it seems as though your reasons for leaving coincide with mine, though we never discussed it at the time and it never occurred to me until right now. I appreciate that you described my actions as brave; but, really, we did the same thing, just at different levels. In general, what is seen as brave is confronting or simply facing the white world day in and day out. That's how the story goes, no? And, I agree that that is the case. But, as you described my case, facing *Black people* and telling our community that we might be wrong for buying into this idea of what knowledge and education should look like or even what kind of life we should strive for itself is unnerving! And, in your case, courage expressed itself at an even deeper level: you had to face *yourself*. Would you agree with that?

SYL: Yes, I think that's a nice way to put it. When I'm asked why I left school, I'm not quite sure how to answer the question. I was in a philosophy program, and philosophy happens to be the worst of all the humanities when it comes to demographics and diversity in the actual views studied. It's understood that in a philosophy department you'll study a lot of white guys. My concentration was on a figure in the history of philosophy, so I went into my MA program well aware that I'd have to read, write about, and become fluent in the views by dead white guys. And, that was the case when I moved to a PhD program, as well. But, I have to admit that it was only when I joined these graduate programs that I felt as though I fit in somewhere for the first time in my life. I finally made close friends, found a suitable mentor, and everything just started to fit together. So, even just in terms of feeling a perfectly natural fit in what's supposed to be a hostile environment, my story diverges quite a bit from most of my friends who are not white or upper-class, and even a bit from yours, Aph. I suppose that I left for existential reasons. I'm a little nervous to put it in those terms. I've been accused of adopting a "post-racial" attitude when I describe my situation that way. Everyone is always waiting to hear about this or that microaggression or a racial (or sexual) harm that I suffered to explain my decision. That sort of racial stuff rarely happened. If anything, it was internal racism eating me up alive that made *any* environment unbearable. I don't know how to describe internalized racism. All I know is that racialized people (especially Black people) are intimately familiar with it and that it is considerably more damaging than police violence, the prison system, lynching, or any other sort of external or institutionalized racism. During my third year of school, I became consumed with the question of how I wanted to live. No matter the answer, I knew I'd have to face this *thing* that I felt inside of me head on. I guess you could call it anti-racist work directed towards the *inside*.

APH: So, I really like how you put this, Syl. Generally, when we think about reasons for why we don't fit in or feel looked down on or uncomfortable, especially in white-dominated spaces, we think the answer lies in confronting the outside or institutional sources of racism (or whatever other -ism is applicable). The assumption is what's *out there* is keeping you "in your place," so to speak. But what you're saying is that although those forces most certainly exist, there is the equally important task of coming to terms with the internalized racism that lurks within each racialized mind/body, which encourages us to self-sabotage even if the environment were ideal. We must confront the colonially imposed inferiority complex.

SYL: Yes. We can't imagine a different future if we are constantly trying to prove that we matter to others . . . and to ourselves. Whether you are in academia is irrelevant. It is strange to me, though, to spend years of my life in "higher education," where searching for a roadmap out of this internal mess is not a priority. What's the point? How does any of this help us face ourselves? What possibility is there for a fulfilling life no matter the paycheck, rank, or location if this is still inside of us? We have to find the strength and courage to say: I'm not going to do this unless this is in the direction of liberation, both in terms of our place in society as well as our souls. And, honestly, I don't think increasing the number of Black people in tenure-track positions has anything to do with that. I mean, it's great if that's happening, but so what? So, that is what I meant when I said that I left for existential reasons.

APH: But, you said you felt like a loser at the start of this conversation.

SYL: I'm a *brave* loser. (laughs)

APH: But, on a serious note, most people whom I would describe as brave don't go around advertising themselves as such.

SYL: That's true. But, I do consider myself to be a very daring person in general and I think this act exemplifies that. Anyway, in your work, you seek to tear down compartments established by arbitrary lines that maintain the status quo. In my work, I seek to tear down psychological compartments established by arbitrary lines that maintain the status quo. Consider the phenomenon of double consciousness famously described by W.E.B. DuBois or sociogeny described by Frantz Fanon. How are these experiences made possible? Well, certain people *created* "Negroes" and "whites" or "American," "French," "African." Now, these are stored in the collective consciousness to benefit certain people and internally wreck certain others. The mere act of dividing people in a specific way gave rise to this. People keep *themselves* in their "place." What would happen if we started all over and drew different lines? Or, no lines at all? And so on and so on. Your work complements mine. Any work that wants to challenge lines like these is courageous work, in my view. But, in looking for an answer to the question, "why was leaving graduate school *brave, per se*," since that is, after all, the theme of this conversation, what do you have to say?

APH: Simply put, it was brave because we did what we wanted to do! School and academia in general wasn't in line with our projects, so we left despite what everyone around us thought or how successful we could have been. "Educated" Black people are so obsessed with respectability that sometimes we forget that being rebels is the only way we'll move forward. I hear a lot of encouragement to be rebels *within* academia. Why not encourage rebellion *about* academia?

8 "You're Doing What?!?"

Leaving Academia to Answer the Call

Roxanna Harlow

I am rational, practical, logical, and risk-averse. I am the opposite of rash. I like to settle into a place, position, and routine. I am shy and introverted. I don't like uncertainty or drastic change. I like to take on challenges that I feel qualified to tackle. My life, therefore, was fairly boring and predictable—until it wasn't.

When I announced that I was leaving academia to start a non-profit organization, almost everyone thought I was crazy. I was a sociology professor at a small liberal arts college where, two years prior, I had become the first African-American woman in the college's history to earn tenure and promotion. I knew nothing about running a non-profit, and I was giving up my career to try. My brother tried to talk sense into me. Levelheaded, practical, and professionally ambitious himself, he couldn't wrap his head around why I would sacrifice everything right when I was on an upward trajectory in my profession. "But you could be department chair in a few years!" he exclaimed, hoping that I would see a reason. More importantly, he was truly worried for me. "How are you going to support yourself?" he wanted to know.

My brother was right, of course—about all of it. I *was* giving up my career. I had no idea how I was going to support myself, though I assumed my savings would last until I found "funding." Social entrepreneurship was completely new to me. "I just want to make sure you've thought this through, because once you leave. . . ." my brother warned, leaving his sentenced unfinished. But I knew how it ended. If I took this step, my traditional career in academia was effectively over.

In 2009, after nine years as a sociology professor, I officially left academia behind and started Higher Learning, Inc., a 501(c)(3) non-profit organization providing low-cost, out-of-school time academic programming for underserved youth ages 11–17. People often describe my decision as "brave," and ask how I got the courage to leave my job. I am never quite sure how to answer this question. I didn't feel particularly brave or courageous. On the contrary, I was full of self-doubt and anxiety. But I was also motivated by a larger force. I didn't *want* to leave the security of my job, yet I felt compelled to act on what every fiber of my being was being called on to do. It's hard to explain unless you've experienced it. *You get to a point where the force driving you forward is stronger than the fear holding you back.*

Some call it God, while others call it a higher power, a spirit, an energy, an instinct, a gut feeling, or all of the above. Whatever that force is, you know it when you feel it. It's especially strong when your life is so out of sync with your needs that you have to either answer the call or pay the price. And so, it happened that I was pulled beyond my own fear into bravery.

On A (Mostly) Traditional Path

My PhD program in sociology trained me to be a researcher, but I realized that my interests lie more with teaching and student development. Therefore, I accepted an offer at a small liberal arts college where teaching was "the first among equals" (of teaching, research, and service). In the summer of 2000, I started my new position as an assistant professor of sociology.

In my first two years at the college, out of a full-time faculty of 100, I was the only tenure-track faculty member on campus who was an African-American woman. In the years after my arrival, I endured the double standards and daily indignities, large and small, which often accompany being one of a few Black (and female) *anything* in a profession. In light of these challenges, my department chair tried her best to be supportive. However, she had no framework for understanding my social position at the college. As a middle-aged white woman, her experience was that students could be jokesters, mischievous, and immature, but they weren't ever malicious, mean, or threatening. She didn't truly understand that, as a young Black woman teaching about social inequality, my reality was completely different from her own. The positive interactions with students, friends, and colleagues helped to offset my day-to-day frustrations, but I still looked forward to the holidays when I would head to my hometown, Chicago, IL, to spend time with family and absorb that wonderful feeling that comes from being around "my people."

During these visits home, my father often talked about the young men living in his high-crime neighborhood on the southwest side of the city. He would share the latest news about the young men he was mentoring or visiting in jail, and express his frustration with the fact that they're industrious and smart, but have few, if any, opportunities to thrive. It struck me particularly hard one day as I watched, for the umpteenth time, teenagers on street corners in the middle of the school day, without hats, coats or gloves. *All of that wasted potential*, I thought. *They're the ones who need me the most.* That feeling stayed with me long after I returned to students complaining about paper assignments or their grades in the class. I was pouring my heart and soul into teaching mostly privileged co-eds who would be just fine, with or without me. Who was supposed to give their heart and soul to those young men in the 'hood?

A year after earning tenure, I took a sabbatical and used that time to do a lot of soul-searching. An expert in the areas of race relations, sociology of education, and social inequality, I ultimately realized that those who could benefit most from my teaching were the students least likely to make it to college. After over a decade teaching the privileged and entitled, I made a decision to serve those who needed me the most and whose futures were integrally tied to mine.

Escaping the Ivory Tower

After much reflection, I decided to start a non-profit educational program to transform the lives of young people of color with little access to the resources critical to success. I had no funding, no base of support, no knowledge of the non-profit sector, and little personal knowledge of the local community I was to serve. But what I *did* know was that for the first time in my life, my work was no longer constrained by an institution designed for and controlled by white people.

As Black women, we often carry around pain and anger from our own oppression along with that of the generations before us. For some of us, it's buried deep within, while for others it hovers perilously close to the surface. In predominantly white and/or male spaces, we may find ourselves in an ongoing struggle to stay respectable (and employed) by keeping our pain and anger in check as we work to ensure equity, justice, and full inclusion for our folk and ourselves. It's a constant hum in the backdrop of our lives as we fight for a space to be Black women, unapologetically, where our hurts, identities, and concerns are acknowledged and centered.

My entire adult life has been structured by institutions, curriculum, expectations, values, and rituals that have little to do with my social history or identity. I have always been fighting against a tide of double standards, exclusion, stereotypes, invisibility, discrimination, and being underestimated, while fighting for justice, representation, and a place of belonging and inclusion— all while keeping the "angry Black woman" out of sight and in check.

By starting my own non-profit, Higher Learning, Inc., I was able to prioritize the needs, histories, and experiences of students of color, design the curriculum with only them in mind, and ignore complaints from middle- and upper-class white parents that my program should be open to "everyone." I didn't have to defend my students' need for a space where they were in the majority and/or where Blackness was valued and validated as a positive part of their identity. I was able to develop my program without tiptoeing around racial minefields or accommodating the demands of white privilege. Creating my own institution, free of that ongoing marginalization, was *liberating*. Armed with my academic skills and a new sense of freedom, drive, and determination, I designed a program that was enriching for my students, their families, and even for me.

Higher Learning, Inc.—The Program

Higher Learning's mission was to provide learning opportunities that move underserved youth beyond familiar boundaries, both mentally and physically, to equip them with the tools and experiences necessary to be successful leaders in their communities, the nation, and the world. Centering the experiences of students of color, the program focused on learning that primarily occurs outside of traditional schooling and is often reserved for families with means. Through discussions, exercises, activities, and travel, we worked to cultivate creative, resourceful, ethical, leaders, thinkers, and problem-solvers. During our summer sessions and various programs throughout the year, students learned within the context of a curricular theme, and had the opportunity to travel abroad.

Our focus on creative and critical thinking, rather than the mechanics of reading and writing, made it easier for all students, whether above or below grade level, to succeed. In fact, for many Higher Learning students, it was the first time they ever excelled at anything academic. For example, I always included a "Student as Teacher Day" in our schedule—a day when students taught about a topic on which they were experts. One of our high school students, who had tested below grade level, wanted to teach about video games. I approved his topic with the caveat that he had to do more than just play the games. I suggested a number of issues for him to think about, such as game violence and quality gamesmanship. Well-practiced in analytical (and sociological) thinking from his years in the program, he assured me that he was on top of it. I was admittedly surprised when he delivered a well-prepared, nuanced presentation, proving that he really *was* on top of it. He discussed many issues, including violence and gender in video games, the culture of gaming, and the mechanics of different types of gaming systems, ending with students taking turns playing games under his direction. He led a college-level discussion—evidence that grade level measures don't always tell us about a person's intelligence or potential.

Other students also flourished. One student was so far *above* grade level that she rarely encountered material in school that challenged her. She thrived in Higher Learning as she soaked up new experiences and fully engaged with college-level ideas (e.g., colonialism and systems of inequality). As a young teen, her aspiration was to become a lawyer. Now a college student, her interests have shifted to international relations and foreign languages—a change she directly attributes to the Higher Learning curriculum, especially her opportunity to travel abroad.

Our students described Higher Learning as "eye-opening," "empowering," and "life-changing." For the 88 percent of our families who were living below the poverty line, the cost was only $35 per year. Parents were grateful that such opportunity-rich yet affordable programs were being offered.

Answering the Call—The Process

When I started Higher Learning, Inc., I encountered many new challenges and learned a great deal along the way. Women of color academics ready to unleash their bravery and pursue an entrepreneurial calling will be pleasantly surprised at how transferable academic skills are to the "real world." I offer the following pieces of advice to help guide the transition.

Dream Big, Start Small

I learned this strategy in graduate school. To avoid becoming paralyzed by the enormity of the project, I divided my dissertation into much smaller pieces, working on it bit by bit until it was done. I utilized this same strategy when I was brainstorming how to start my own enterprise. My first idea was to start a school, but it quickly became clear that a school was too large of an undertaking for me to launch alone. The thought of it overwhelmed me, so I broke my idea down into smaller, more manageable pieces. Given my lack of economic and human capital, a better starting point was a small summer program.

I started Higher Learning with only fifteen middle school and nine high school students. We made do with chairs and tables in a conference room, chart paper instead of a chalkboard, a stretch of grass for a lunchroom, and carpooling for field trips. Six years later, we expanded to six different programs, served over 300 students, and developed eight partnerships. Our students visited twelve colleges, attended conferences, and traveled to three different countries.

I recommend starting with what you *can* do, with the resources you *do* have, and build from there. If you wait for everything to be perfect or set your sights too high, you'll never get started. You will feel overwhelmed by the enormity of the task. *How do you eat an elephant? One bite at a time.*

Use What You Know and What You Love in What You Do

After I left academia, people often asked me whether I missed sociology, or regretted "wasting" my degree, or if I was planning to "go back into" teaching. I have always found these questions frustratingly odd. Higher Learning allowed me to teach sociology in an applied way to young people who could use that information to make a difference in their lives. I'm not a certified elementary or secondary school teacher, so I moved beyond that traditional format and developed a different type of curriculum focused on educating young people through sociology.

My students and I tackled issues such as environmental justice, poverty, social change, cultural and religious differences, and economic and political systems. I never stopped teaching sociology nor being a sociologist. In many ways, I was doing more with my PhD than I had before—I was putting it into practice! My vision for Higher Learning was based entirely on my training, experience, what I know and what I love. I never left the discipline, just the traditional format for engaging with it. When developing your idea, don't worry about what's usually expected. Implement it in a way that capitalizes on your skills, talents, and interests.

Research, Write, Assess!

Entrepreneurs need research skills because they always need to research, assess, and write up information about their business. I had to do research on market needs, becoming a tax-exempt non-profit, and managing middle and high school students. I had to find and apply for grants, do program assessments, write up annual reports, and much more.

I originally planned to establish Higher Learning in a large city instead of the small town where I live. However, I discovered that the local Black and Latino students, similar to young people in urban areas, fell significantly behind their white peers not only academically, but also on measures of social well-being. Further, while the larger city had a variety of educational programs for underserved students, there were no such programs in my county. Therefore, I began Higher Learning locally, and expanded it later. It was a good thing I did my research first.

Save Money and Forget the Lawyer

For anyone who's had to analyze Max Weber, plow through Emile Durkheim, or decipher post-modernist theory, interpreting the legalese you encounter on various documents and government forms is child's play. I didn't realize, until I started filing applications for non-profit status (which is *really* simple), and 501(c)(3) tax-exempt status (which is more tedious), that the reading and analytical skills I gained from engaging with difficult texts in sociology also taught me strategies for deciphering almost anything.

Experience with dense textual analysis minimizes the intimidation factor associated with complex forms. I began to think, if I can figure out Michel Foucault, then surely, I can figure out how to file this paperwork, right? If you have the time and patience, are practiced at cutting through confusing language, and are good with details and directions, you can save money on a lawyer and probably do most start-up (and most other!) paperwork yourself.

Expect Stress

There is a great deal of stress involved in running your own enterprise. This is the case with any new undertaking; however, the nature of entrepreneurship includes financial insecurity. Even if you are flush with resources, your revenue stream is not guaranteed. After I left my tenured faculty position,

I had no health insurance, no dental care, no vision care, no income flow, and no retirement contributions (as I had no salary). Without children, I didn't qualify for Medicaid or many other types of welfare, and I owned a home, thus making me ineligible for food stamps. I relied on the free clinic for health care and the local food pantry for food.

It was in the freedom of self-determination that I found the bravery required to sacrifice my financial security and dignity for Higher Learning, Inc. The need to offer a validating educational experience for my students, without concern for accommodating white interests, was powerful. I had no dependents, so I was able to make that choice. However, if your family depends on your paycheck, then you may want to try to accomplish your goals while remaining in a paid position.

There's No Shame in Having a Safety Net

In light of the financial risks, I recommend that you consider working under the umbrella of a well-established organization. For example, you could start your enterprise with the backing of your college or university—this is a good way to maintain financial stability while building your business. Or, you could see whether another non-profit will take you and your work under their wing. This allows you to start fundraising under a tax-exempt institution, and funders are more likely to invest in you while you are under a reputable umbrella. I wanted to maintain full autonomy and control over my organization's programs, so launching out on my own was the right decision for Higher Learning. However, working within an existing institution, even for the short-term, can be a great way to get established and build a reputation with fewer risks.

Get to Know Your Client Base

Leaving the "ivory tower" was like having blinders removed. I discovered that I knew nothing about the community in which I lived. I joined the boards of local organizations, and spent a lot of time going to church services and community gatherings in an effort to learn about the area, get to know people, and have them get to know me. In addition to identifying supporters and potential partners, I learned a great deal about the challenges our students faced, from transportation issues to ongoing family turmoil. I also discovered a division between "native" Black families who'd lived in the area for generations and Black "transplants" who'd moved from other cities, states, and countries.

As a light-skinned Black "transplant" and a professor connected to the local college, I was viewed with skepticism by many lower-income Black "native" residents who had good reason to be wary of anyone associated with white educational establishments. Although we built some trust, Higher Learning remained most popular with Black "transplants" from larger cities and other countries. The time I spent learning about the community was invaluable to my ability to serve the students in my program. It also made me aware of the need to develop strategies for breaking down barriers created by my own privilege.

"Just When I Thought I Was Out, They Pull Me Back In"

My non-profit continued to grow each year. However, one challenge that I was unable to surmount was the difficulty of securing a sustainable funding source. There simply wasn't enough revenue to support a salary; I relied on volunteers alone. All revenue went to student programs and basic organizational expenses. After all of my savings and half of my retirement account were exhausted, I obtained multiple part-time jobs while also running Higher Learning. However, the more work I took on, the less time I had to devote to the program. Eventually, the situation became untenable, and after six incredible years of educating young people, we held our final summer session in 2014. In 2015, we shifted away from direct service to use our remaining resources for grants and scholarships for Higher Learning students and alumni.

More than a year before our final end-of-term reception, I knew that without major funders, I would soon have to shut down the program. So, when the time came to say goodbye, I was ready. I was upset, however, for the many students and parents who depended on Higher Learning for summer enrichment. For many of them, Higher Learning was their "family"—a place of belonging for mostly Black teens in a predominately white, conservative county. Parents and students alike expressed sadness and disappointment. But I could no longer deliver the program and keep a roof over my head, so it was time for me to find another way to do this type of meaningful work.

I became excited about transitioning into the foundation sector; I wanted to work for a grant-making foundation to identify organizations doing great work, assess proposals, and fund them. However, I was unable to break into that market, and I had similarly poor luck with my applications to direct service non-profits. Even so, when a full-time sociology position opened up at the local community college, I had no intention of applying—I didn't want to go back into academia! However, my ever-sensible brother convinced me to submit an application, arguing that applying would at least give me options. I took his advice, was offered the position, and became a full-time member of the faculty in August 2016.

The students at community colleges tend to be quite different, on the whole, from those at four-year liberal arts schools. I find the students to be more varied in age, social class, interests, and life experiences—and I like that. However, I once again find myself having to conform and cater to the needs and sensibilities of white students and administrators in a predominantly white institution while challenging the structures of inequality.

Working at the college while remaining involved with local community organizations means that I now have one foot in academia with the other still in non-profit/service/advocacy/activism work. Whether I can carve out a niche where I can pursue my goals while also serving the needs of the institution remains to be seen.

Conclusion

"But you're happy, right?" This question would often follow an exchange that went something like "Hi, Rox! How've you been? How's Higher Learning?" I would then respond by mentioning our programs along with my ongoing struggle for funding. While hearing about my financial difficulties, it seemed to make people feel better to know that at least I was *happy*. But it wasn't a good question to ask; it is like asking someone with a new restaurant if they are happy while they're working 18-hour days and not yet turning a profit.

I was frustrated, overworked, managing teens and tweens, and stressed by the everyday worries of making ends-meet while living below the poverty line. So, no—I wasn't happy. The better question to ask would have been, "Are you doing what you want to do? Are you whole and fulfilled?" And to that, I would have easily answered "Yes!"

Periodically, I'm asked whether I regret my decision to leave academia. My answer is a resounding, unequivocal "NO!" Not one iota. I am proud of the positive influence Higher Learning, Inc. has had on students' lives. We changed each other in the best of ways. Former Higher Learning students and alumni now drop by my office at the college to catch up and reminisce. Parents continue to ask if we'll start up again. It's those times when my certainty that I made the right decision is validated. I was lucky to work with amazing groups of young people. They touched me deeply as I watched them grow personally, socially, and intellectually.

We need to ask ourselves what we want our life and legacy to be, then work toward making that happen, even when it conflicts with the expectations others may have and hope for us. *That* is truly brave. For some of us, our bravery is expressed through our work to change institutions from within. For some, it's leaving the traditional path to seek alternative solutions. For others it's something else altogether. For me, as I turn another page in my life, it's staying true to myself while having a positive impact in whatever way I can, wherever I am.

Acknowledgments

I would like to thank Anna Kuang for keeping me sane. She serves as my "anger translator," openly expressing the emotion and frustration that I am required to bury.

Part II
Collective Resistance
Counternarratives to the Ethos of Individualistic Meritocracy in the Academy

9 Love Note

Robbin Chapman

There is nothing to fear
I am cherished, nurtured, stronger
Forged in the blood, sweat, and grace of my elders
Who carved a passage just for me
Enslaved Inventors, Sisters, Sharecroppers, Activists
Brutalized Musicians, Grandparents, Poets, Students
Raped Teachers, Brothers, Maids, Storytellers
Lynched Scientists, Children, Janitors, Artists
A brave multitude enduring, defying, surviving
the *unSpeakable*
Without their boldness, bending, and tenacity
I would not, could not
thrive, disrupt, persist
@ MIT

10 *La Colectiva*

Peer Mentoring on the Path to Thrival

Mariela Nuñez-Janes, Amelia M. Kraehe, Andrea Silva, Alicia Re Cruz, Bertina H. Combes, and Valerie Martinez-Ebers

On the album *Siempre viviré*, released three years before her death, Cuban salsa queen Celia Cruz recorded a song inspired by Gloria Gaynor's hit "I Will Survive" (Fekaris, Perren, & Gomez Diaz, 2000). Celia Cruz's version of survival is a call to crossing borders and shattering barriers: "*Rompiendo barreras voy sobreviviendo/Cruzando fronteras voy sobreviviendo.*" Being a woman of color in the academy is—like Celia Cruz's interpretation of Gaynor's lyrics—an exercise in *sobrevivencia* (survival). Despite the individualism that pervades academe, survival requires collective efforts to thrive personally and professionally. What possibilities emerge when faculty who are women of color work together to ensure their individual and collective survival? What does thrival look like when it becomes a collective endeavor? In this essay, we present a peer mentoring model specifically for women of color scholars who collectively ensure one another's success and well-being in the academy by providing professional and personal support.

We—a diverse group of women of color faculty at the University of North Texas (UNT) from varying ranks and academic backgrounds—created and implemented a peer mentoring group we call *La Colectiva*. In coming together as women of color faculty in a predominantly white institution, we challenge the neoliberal university's emphasis on individualism and its limited notions of productivity and inclusiveness. Our model of faculty peer mentoring is fluid and shaped by our professional and personal experiences as we negotiate the obstacles of promotion, tenure, departmental and university politics, as well as the trials and tribulations in our roles as mothers, daughters, and partners to our loved ones. Through *La Colectiva*, we are able to grow as individuals through conversations that recognize the full array of our personal, professional, and departmental challenges. Connecting our divergent experiences is professionally rewarding and personally healing because we are able to engage our common condition as women of color in the academy and challenge oppressing institutional barriers that ignore or silence our humanity.

Beyond the supportive space we have created within *La Colectiva*, our efforts have been important for carving out space for women of color throughout the campus. At the time that we formally created *La Colectiva*, less than one percent of faculty at UNT were women of color—70 percent of whom were untenured. The vast majority of full professors were non-Hispanic white men. As women of color faculty, claiming a space at the intersections of race and gender in a predominantly white institution was necessary and urgent. We knew that the conversations in which we engaged at university events, between classes, and before and after committee meetings were important to our visibility, if not acceptance among non-Hispanic white faculty. Yet, we recognized that greater visibility was also necessary to push our departments, colleges, and university to acknowledge our presence and contributions and to push for systemic inclusion and equity.

Our collective purpose is to provide personal and professional support, and to enhance the professional development of women of color at UNT through an emphasis on tenure, promotion, research, and teaching. We work collectively to pursue the following goals, which are more fully elaborated later in this chapter:

- help each member of *La Colectiva* navigate tenure and promotion successfully
- mentor and support new women of color faculty to acclimate to departmental and institutional politics
- build relationships that are personally and academically empowering
- provide emotional support to fellow *La Colectiva* members as we navigate challenges of our professional and personal roles
- and, advocate for infrastructure to support women of color faculty.

The primary actions associated with achieving our goals are highlighted in Figure 10.1.

Group Structure

What distinguishes us from other faculty mentoring groups on our campus is our holistic approach and our multiracial and transcultural membership. In forming *La Colectiva*, we recognized the necessity for an intellectual space of shared expertise, so we thought it was important to be inclusive with respect to disciplines and ranks. Thus, our initial group included five self-identified Latinas (two assistant professors, one associate professor, and two full professors), who represented two colleges and four disciplines. We now have ten members (either Black or Latina) who continue to represent a variety of disciplines covering the social sciences and humanities. New members were identified through our existing network and referred by other women in the group or through contact at public events. Relying on our own networking efforts was critical to our effort to claim our own space by building both intersectional and interdisciplinary relationships as the strategic focus of our expansion. We identify members and build affinities

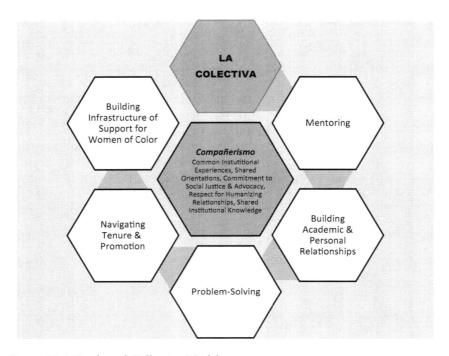

Figure 10.1 Goals and Collective Model

through *compañerismo* and sisterhood—bonds of fictive kinship and solidarity that result from: 1) common experiences of institutional racism and
sexism; 2) shared philosophical orientations; 3) a commitment to social justice and advocacy; 4) the respect for humanizing relationships as scholars
and educators; and, 5) a shared sense of institutional knowledge.

Collectively, we identify knowledge and wisdom in common experiences
of racism, sexism, and tokenism, and honor the work of other mentoring
groups on campus like the Black Women's Initiative and the Women's Faculty Network. As we work through these affinities, we share our knowledge
with other women of color faculty outside of our group through public lectures, fora, and networking with similar mentoring groups. For example, we
participate in events sponsored by other faculty mentoring programs that
are inclusive of all women; we also coordinate strategies and organize fora
that address the concerns of women faculty of color on campus.

But our bi-weekly meetings are structured around our unique priorities
and needs. We use storytelling to express and sustain our *compañerismo*
and sisterhood. Storytelling is critical for generating the collective knowledge of the group so that we may understand each other's realities and
work together to imagine and advocate for alternative systems in which the

intellectual and creative work of women of color can flourish and be valued. To tell one's story is to reveal oneself and become vulnerable. In any setting, this can feel dangerous, but particularly so in the academy. An academic is trained to critique others' ideas, to identify the failings of others' methods, and to defend her own. The collective courage to trust and rely on each other is the backbone of *La Colectiva*. This holistic, humanizing approach encourages us as we take steps, big and small, for a more just and inclusive university. It recognizes our individual labor and roles in the academy intersectionally while also acknowledging that success is a group effort. Annually, we identify a point person who is charged with scheduling meetings and managing our small annual budget. We have realized that it is important to assign this task to tenured women or those who have submitted their materials for promotion and tenure because of the responsibility and the pressure to "publish or perish" for those who are on the tenure-track.

Each meeting is a one-and-a-half to two-hour conversation that begins with identifying who has urgent concerns and who needs immediate feedback. In some instances, we have used a rating scale that we developed to help each of us identify our priorities to the group. In other cases, we simply start our meeting with each of us stating whether we have individual questions or issues that we need to discuss with our group. In addition to this, we circulate an agenda prior to our meetings to outline items for collective discussion. These include reminders of events of interest, discussing nominations for campus awards, addressing logistics relevant to our own sponsored lectures or gatherings.

Ensuring Thrival in the Academy

Navigating Tenure and Promotion Successfully

La Colectiva provides a space to support women of color on the track to tenure and promotion because it allows us to access and share our collective professional wisdom. Since the formation of *La Colectiva*, all of the tenure-track members have achieved successful third-year reviews or earned tenure, and one associate professor was promoted to full professor and subsequently appointed to an academic dean's position. During the 2015–2016 academic year, we collectively published eleven articles in peer-reviewed journals, had two books accepted for publication and one published, submitted one book manuscript for review, and hosted two solo art exhibitions. In addition, multiple members earned university and national recognition for their scholarship, in some cases, after having been successfully nominated by *La Colectiva*.

Collectively, we have accomplished so much by structuring our meetings around our professional priorities. At the beginning of the semester, we share our individual goals for the academic year; during our meetings, we regularly follow-up on progress towards our stated individual goals. We also read and comment on each other's materials before they are submitted for peer-review, which encourages a focus on scholarship. Sometimes this process is formalized, as when some of the tenure-track women in *La Colectiva* organized a writing group where they met at a local coffee shop to work on a regular basis on their manuscripts. We also invite senior scholars to campus to meet with our tenure-track faculty members to provide feedback on their projects. Contact with highly esteemed scholars whose research agendas align with ours also lends added symbolic weight to our individual scholarship and our collective work. Most importantly, our junior faculty members feel the wider net of support in and out of our own university.

Bertina's story highlights how membership in *La Colectiva* has strengthened her ability to receive and provide feedback:

> *After asking senior members of* La Colectiva *to review my work for consideration for promotion to full professor, some came back with hard questions. Initially, I felt sad and perhaps even a bit hurt by their critique. However, careful consideration encouraged me to be brave enough to accept the honest review of others. I was able to make some necessary adjustments to my own dossier and better prepare myself for submission. Conversely, when opportunities have arisen to review the work of others within* La Colectiva *and faculty and women of color outside the group, I have become more confident in reviewing and responding honestly. Yes, inequity, sexism, oppression, and racism do exist in the academy and women faculty and/or faculty of color are frequently the targets. However, honesty and bravery are critical, especially when I believe these negative factors may not be present.*

Mentoring New Faculty

For *La Colectiva* members who are just beginning their academic careers, the group has served as a lifeline during the difficult transition to a new institution—particularly one where there are so few fellow women of color. We co-create a space where one is free from being "the only" one and doubting oneself and being doubted by others. For example, Amelia notes:

> *When I started as a faculty member at UNT, I solicited advice from experienced professors, many of them from other universities. The advice I received was to keep my head down, don't say anything, and stay away from my campus as much as possible. I sought out guidance through new faculty sessions at conferences. At one of these, a renowned white woman professor led the group of mostly young faculty of color in meditative exercises as rehearsal for how to emotionally and psychologically disengage during department faculty meetings. This struck me as odd until I learned that some faculty employ pharmaceuticals just to navigate workplace politics and hostilities. These*

early lessons were clear and yet full of contradiction—survival in the academy would require that I disappear, erasing myself and any aspect of my humanity that might attract attention. La Colectiva *is where I am recognized as a full, multidimensional being. I am supported with strategies for speaking up and making sure my voice is heard in situations where it matters. We relate to each other on an equal footing in* La Colectiva, *each woman serving as a role model for each other despite our vast differences in individual backgrounds and life experiences. It is from seeing Valerie, Mariela, Bertina, Andrea, Alicia and other fellow Colectivistas' demonstrations of strength and fortitude that I have summoned my own personal courage to move beyond a head down mode of academic survival.*

Andrea expressed a similar sentiment about the support she's received from our peer mentoring group:

La Colectiva *has provided me a ready support system for my first year as an assistant professor at a Research I university. My graduate school experience lacked mentoring or support opportunities from other women of color. As a result, I learned to second guess my skills and ideas. I thought my work and suggestions were not as valuable as my other colleagues.* La Colectiva *created a built-in group of women of color from various departments and levels of tenure and promotion. These women had also been subjected to the same obstacles and institutional racism I encountered during my graduate program and in my new institution. More than anything, the women from* La Colectiva *were the first group of women who had experienced the obstacles I was facing first hand. They had navigated the road I have begun walking and gave me their suggestions based on their experiences. The support and encouragement I get from these women has made me brave. I trust these women with my hopes and fears and they have handled them with care. More than this, they have encouraged me when I felt I was struggling, they have led me when I felt lost, and they have supported me when I've felt alone. The simple act of empathy and mentorship has encouraged me to continue working in academia, knowing I have a group of women who have worked through my struggles.*

Empowerment

La Colectiva fosters a sense of collective bravery, while facilitating each member's personal bravery, as well. What constitutes bravery in our collective and individual acts is a willingness to take on difficult issues when entrusted with a position of power and authority and to institutionalize systematic change. This collective space allows us to speak up, speak against, or speak within departmental, administrative meetings, or classrooms.

Through our group we are able to share strategies, come up with language to articulate and challenge microaggressions and institutional violence, and learn what has worked or not for others. In a tokenized environment with so few women of color, the act of gathering safely as a collective feels liberating, defiant, and empowering.

Alicia's personal story is one of empowerment through her membership in *La Colectiva:*

> *Sharing our stories through our conversations at* La Colectiva *meetings has a profound impact for me, particularly in pushing me to revisit past events in my life when I felt awkward, confused and/or different. It was through these meetings that I started the process of becoming aware of microaggressions. To find the words and concepts to put meaning into those feelings was liberating and empowering. Not that long ago, I witnessed the power for action, the bravery resulting from my awareness of microaggresions. As a member of a professional organization, I was recognized publicly for my service at a professional meeting. The PowerPoint slide listed my first name, Alicia, with the last name of another Latina member of the organization. In other words, the name resulted from the combination of the names of two different Latina members. This symbolically made both of us invisible as active members and reduced us to fictive "Latina Members" of the organization. It was painful, to say the least, to know that what was supposed to be a public recognition of service, encapsulated in a name, became identified with a no-name or, better said, a fictive name made out of two Latina names. Before my experience as a* La Colectiva *member, I might have channeled the pain through the psychological strategy of forcing myself to believe that "it was just a mistake." However, it was the experiential knowledge of our Colectiva conversations that encouraged me to write a statement addressed to the president of the organization, in which I pointed out the unconscious bias, structural contradictions, and tokenism embedded in "that mistake."*

Valerie also notes finding confidence as a member of *La Colectiva:*

> *Being in* La Colectiva *finally made me realize that I am not an imposter! Talking with my fellow Colectivistas, I discovered that they struggle with similar insecurities. Collectively, we found more effective ways to survive and thrive as minority women in academia rather than just keeping our heads down and "going along" as I had been doing. Now, I speak up when I disagree with departmental actions and I am getting better at saying no to every service request. Moreover, because members of* La Colectiva *frequently ask and follow my advice, I gained confidence in both my scholarship and leadership abilities.*

Emotional Support

La Colectiva is often where the healing starts for members of the group. It is the space colored by the condition of liberation, for us ignited by the act of *com-prender* built through our conversational interactions. Academia targets pieces of us when addressing our differences. The result is an alienated self, fragmented in pieces that do not fit the institutional normalizing order. And, this fragmented self-hurts. This is why *La Colectiva* meetings are so important; they create a soothing, healing, and safe place.

Mariela reflects on a time when she found support that she urgently needed during a *La Colectiva* meeting:

> *The supportive collective space of* La Colectiva *was integral to my ability to cope with my father's cancer diagnosis, hospice, and death while I juggled my professional duties and my role as a mother of a young child. I learned about my dad's diagnosis with stage four kidney cancer during one of* La Colectiva's *bi-weekly meetings. I was expecting a call from my brother and stepped outside to hear about the findings of tests that I knew were definitive. Although my dad was in his early eighties, the advanced stage of the cancer was surprising news because my dad had received a clean bill of health up to that point. Instead of wiping my tears and excusing myself from the meeting—a strategy I would have used in different circumstances—I walked back to the meeting returning to the conversation again with tears still flowing from my eyes. In this instance, and during the progress of my father's disease, talking about the mixed emotions, the practicalities of caring for a loved one long-distance, the emotional weight of doing life while seeing death, were topics of discussion that were just as important, and in some cases even more important, than discussing the progress of a manuscript or the challenges of getting through a full teaching and service load.* La Colectiva *provided a safe space to cope and acknowledge my pain as a daughter and my roles as mother and professor, while also functioning as a productive faculty member. Because of* La Colectiva, *I am confident that my humanity—my pain, my joy, my intellect—and not just my labor, are integral to my scholarship and teaching.*

Advocate for Infrastructure to Support Women of Color Faculty

While ensuring that our own professional success is a priority, we also regularly discuss what is happening at our university and organize explicitly to have a voice and influence the decision-making process. We determine the priorities that we want to present to our administration. In this regard, we collaborated with other faculty groups to organize a meeting with our university's president that would raise awareness about issues that are important to us. One example of this was suggesting to our president the possibility of institutional membership in the National Center for Faculty Development and Diversity (NCFDD). Individual faculty had purchased membership and found participation useful. However, the high cost of membership became prohibitive. *La Colectiva* requested a meeting to explain the benefits and possible outcomes of a university investment. Following our meeting, we collaborated with the Black Faculty Network, who also met with the president. The outcome of our collective efforts was an institutional membership that proved useful for all faculty and graduate students and, in some colleges and schools at the university, provided critical sources of mentoring support for new faculty.

La Colectiva has also committed to creating space to feature scholarship on and about women of color. We organized an array of campus events with invited women of color scholars from outside our university who present their work in university-wide lectures. At a basic level, this networking helps increase awareness among our colleagues who may not be familiar with the subject matter, theories, or methods with which *La Colectiva* members are professionally engaged. We also organized a local conference on tokenism in the academy open to faculty and administrators and, during our third-year, organized a lecture series by members of *La Colectiva* featuring our scholarly projects. This is significant because our university, until now, has done very little to promote the scholarship of women of color and has had few discussions about racism and discrimination within the institution. These projects bring our issues out of the shadows and into the center of campus life, but on our own terms.

Concluding Words of Collective Wisdom

La Colectiva reflects a collective model for thriving and courage among women of color in the academy and beyond. Thrival is difficult to achieve when, individually, we often feel that we are merely surviving; but it is crucial that we thrive in the face of institutional as well as personal challenges. Although there are many forces that seem beyond our control and insurmountable given the litany of daily responsibilities to which we must attend, it is all the more important that we internalize the assumption that our failures and accomplishments are not solely dependent on our individual efforts. The way we survive—and *thrive*—is by relying on each other. It takes courage to ask for help, it takes bravery to reach our hands to the ones who are left behind, and it takes a combined effort to sustain this work to thrust all of us forward, together, collectively.

Reference

Fekaris, D., Perren, F., & Gomez Diaz, O. (2000). Yo viviré (I will survive) [Recorded by C. Cruz]. *On Siempre viviré* [MP 3 file]. Sonic Music Entertainment.

11 Fiery Mind, Full Heart, Brave Soul

A Model for Women of Color to Thrive in Historically White Colleges and Universities

Robbin Chapman

Introduction

As an African-American woman academic, I compare my traversal of Historically White Colleges and Universities (HWCUs) to that of someone maneuvering a maze of smoke and mirrors. I experience either hyper-attentiveness to my every behavior or hyper-invisibility that shrouds and dismisses me as a scholar and a person. I have had these kinds of experiences throughout my academic career, from my undergraduate studies to the present as an administrator and faculty member. However, in drawing strength and courage from my ancestors and elders, I recently became proactive in taking ownership and authorship of my growth as a scholar, teacher, intellectual, and lifelong learner. In particular, I developed a model for professional development specifically for women of color academics like myself to thrive in the academy, especially in HWCUs. The purpose of this essay is to share this model, which I call the Thrive Mosaic, in hopes of supporting fellow women of color scholars.

Origins of the Thrive Mosaic

From student, to faculty, to administrator, I have experienced being "othered" as an African-American woman at every step of my career in academia. I have endured microaggressions fueled by tired stereotypes, which in turn, serve to justify discrimination and domination. My success in elite white-dominated academic spaces has been viewed as a threat by some. I have had to work harder to receive less, if any, respect and recognition, been overlooked for the leadership opportunities that my white and male peers were granted, and have had to push back against being tokenized. While painful, I realize that my experiences are neither unique nor exceptional. I have witnessed too many talented scholars of color enduring similarly painful experiences. Our ongoing struggle to advance our academic agendas while preserving our dignity often requires making a choice between raising our voices or staying silent. Giving voice too often renders us disregarded and isolated, readily labeled the "angry Black woman." Staying silent, we become frustrated and drained. These conditions are exacerbated when access and opportunity in academia are steeped in the dominant and often white culture of the academy.

Early in my academic career, I often failed to take advantage of professional opportunities when I didn't know what to expect as a first-generation academic. Other times, I let others discourage me from getting all to which I was entitled. Through experience, I began to recognize the ways in which scholars of color lose out professionally due to limited access to crucial professional networks—in part, because of external threats like racism and sexism and, in part, because we simply fail to develop and leverage our networks to excel. This is why cultivating a specialized network of people—from various disciplines and positions of power—with a demonstrated fluency in culturally competent practices is crucial if women of color scholars are to thrive in the academy.

I was awarded a Ford Foundation fellowship for my graduate studies and was grateful for this financial support because it gave me more freedom to explore my research interests. However, the real treasures of the fellowship were the relationships I developed with other Ford Fellows. My first Conference of Ford Fellows and every subsequent gathering inspired me to persist and to resist in hostile academic spaces. Ford Fellows are mostly underrepresented scholars, many of whom have had similar experiences of marginalization and of working towards social justice in the academy. I could ask any Ford Fellow for advice or mentoring without having to justify or convince them of the aggressions to which I am subjected in my academic institution. I can trust them to advise me well, especially on specific issues like navigating the challenges of inhabiting HWCU spaces as an African-American woman. Over the years, they have served as my mentors, advocates, accountability partners, and have contributed to my professional development as a leader and a scholar. This amazing network of scholars of color was my inspiration for developing a coherent network-based model for professional development.

Moving forward on my academic journey, I wanted to have access to the opportunities afforded my white, male peers and that I realized would be essential to my success. I knew that meant cultivating specialized relationships, specifically connections that are race-aware and open to discussions of privilege, power, and oppression. Drawing upon my unique assets, I developed a tool for professional development for women of color academics, which I call the Thrive Mosaic. The Mosaic positions me to observe, connect, reflect, and act on lessons learned through my experiences in the academy and from the experiences of credible others.

The Thrive Mosaic Scholar Development Framework

The Thrive Mosaic is a professional development tool designed specifically for women of color scholars working at HWCUs. It is a framework for cultivating specialized relationships that are race-aware, honoring of one's cultural assets, and that provide advocacy and other supports. Given the futility of waiting for predominantly white institutions and their agents to increase their cultural competency and engage in more equitable practices, this model allows women of color to take ownership and authorship of their growth and success in academia.

The Thrive Mosaic is a powerful and specialized network of people who are thinking about how their social justice activism can mitigate oppression and other challenges scholars of color encounter in the academy. What distinguishes the Mosaic from "race-neutral" professional networks is the nuanced awareness and understanding of the implications of race and gender in professional relationships. It is imperative that the people you bring into your Mosaic network understand the implications of race and gender for your professional growth. Engaging across racial and gender lines in academia occurs against a national backdrop of race-mattering, and white and male privilege. This can diminish the value of women and people of color when privileged norms are the measure of competence and authority. Thus, awareness and understanding the implications of race and gender are critical skills for those relationships in your Thrive Mosaic.

The Mosaic is comprised of six distinct roles: 1) associates, 2) advocates, 3) connectors, 4) mentors, 5) coaches, and 6) targeted training. Figure 11.1 (below) displays the roles that comprise the Mosaic. In what follows, I discuss each of the six roles in greater detail.

Figure 11.1 Thrive Mosaic Scholar Development Framework

Associate

Associates are mutual accountability partners. They help you to set realistic goals, refine your process for scholarly production, and provide feedback and encouragement on specific projects. This is a reciprocal relationship in which both parties monitor and insist on scholarly progression or reevaluation of current scholarly objectives. Working with my associates over the years has increased my awareness and control of my strategies for productive, scholarly action. The power of this trusted, collegial relationship is that you engage in explicit and regular episodes of reflection on your learning and scholarship processes (writing, research, teaching, and leadership) within the context of your current professional goals. Associates give honest, constructive feedback even when it may be difficult to hear. This is a high-trust relationship that sets high expectations because you are sharing and analyzing your weaknesses and uncertainties.

Let me provide a personal example of how I discovered the power of associates. As Black graduate students at MIT, my friends and I created a support group called the Academy of Courageous Minority Engineers (ACME). The ACME meetings (named "Accountability Thursdays") were our time to focus on crafting strategies for negotiating racially hostile spaces, moving our graduate work forward toward completion, and helping one another grapple with fears that might have prevented us from taking that next brave step forward. The kinds of encouraging words that I heard from my peers included: "Yes, you're going back into the lab, even though this racist incident happened." "Yes, you're going to make that thesis proposal deadline." "Yes, I will meet you and we can work on our writing together." "Let's figure out what still needs to get done and put together a schedule with check-ins." "Yes, it is okay that you take care of yourself and get some sleep. We will wake you up and make sure you get back to work." Our group of courageous minority engineers looked out for each other with compassion, honesty, and high expectations for success. We were accountable to one another, and we were brave, together.

ACME peers emphasized the importance of systematic progress and acknowledging milestones. One of our members developed a software program (this was MIT, after all) specifically for project management and tracking goal progression. This enabled us to check-in online, track progress, share our thoughts, and "look in" on how others were faring. We could quickly identify when one of us was struggling and "check-in" immediately rather than wait for the weekly in-person gatherings. This combination of high trust, cultural sensitivity, and high expectations created a relationship in which we began to understand each of our particular processes for productive scholarship. Doing this "meta-scholar" thinking in conjunction with other Black graduate students became an important source of bravery for me, especially when I was experiencing self-doubt. All of us experienced those moments. But we were an alliance. And we succeeded, together. We are still a community, even years after graduating from MIT. The critical thinking, the strategizing to overcome obstacles, the camaraderie, the encouragement, and looking out for one another was our training ground for success. Today, I have well over seventy associates, all trusted colleagues, from across every academic discipline, industry, government, and beyond. They are a continual source of courage through encouragement and accountability.

Advocate

An *advocate* is a colleague who is in a position to promote your strengths and accomplishments and to support your professional advancement. Advocates are neither mentors nor advisors. They need not be in your field or discipline. However, they should be able to speak credibly about your work, write letters of support, and nominate you for awards, appointments, and leadership opportunities. Your responsibility to your advocates is to update them about your accomplishments annually or when a major milestone occurs. This type of communication ensures that they can speak about your potential, speak out against racialized or gendered assumptions of your work or career pathways, and look for opportunities that are typically inaccessible or denied to women of color scholars. You should look for advocates with color insight, who can work to ensure that you have access to the same opportunities being made available to others. They should be aware that women of color are systematically excluded and denied opportunities in academia and, as such, should work on your behalf to aid you in overcoming these obstacles.

Advocates have been critical to my own leadership development and advancement as an African-American woman academic. My white colleagues often do not see me as a strong candidate for advancement and leadership opportunities. My advocates have been critical agents in diminishing such obstacles. They use their power and position to ensure that the proper inquiries are made and resources redirected when necessary. For example, one of my advocates is a highly respected, African-American male sociologist. We have discussed how he might be a strong advocate on my behalf and decided that he would look for academic opportunities for me where there is little to no representation of African-American women. He has nominated me to speak on panels at engineering society conferences (i.e., ASEE) and more recently for a Sigma XI Distinguished Lectureship. Another advocate, who has served in this role since graduate school, is a white woman education professor at the University of Pennsylvania. She has used her influence to appoint me as co-editor on a book entitled *The Computer Clubhouse: Constructionism and Creativity in Youth Communities*, and has put my name forth to give lectures and deliver keynote addresses. We talk often about how women can support one another and how white women can use their race privilege to remove obstacles and provide opportunities for women of color in the academy.

Connector

A *connector* has access to credible and influential networks (either broadly or in a particular area of focus) and can facilitate connecting you to relevant people or privileged networks. You should establish a broad collection of connectors from a variety of academic, leadership, and professional backgrounds. Having connections to an array of professional networks is an important factor in networking opportunities. It is not necessary for connectors to have a high level of cultural competency; however, it is helpful for connectors to be aware of the networks from which you are typically excluded because of your race and/or gender. Over time, these new connectors can shift to the other, more intense and high-trust relationships in your Mosaic network.

Let me share an example of how I utilized a connector to advance my goal of promoting inclusion. Several years ago, one of my connectors, a visiting ACE Fellow, facilitated my access to the MIT Chair of the Corporation (similar to the chair of a Board of Trustees). I hoped to discuss with the Chair how the departmental visiting committees might help drive a department-level diversity agenda. I had spent the prior year unsuccessfully trying to get on the Chair's calendar. I simply had no access to that level of leadership. My connector, an African-American woman and law professor, had access to his office and was able to break through the red tape. I used that meeting to secure several subsequent discussions with the Chair and work with him to enhance the visiting committee training program. Our efforts resulted in the addition of "diversity probes" into visiting committee's portfolio of questions, incentivizing departments to make credible progress with their diversity and inclusion goals.

Mentor

Mentors fall in two broad categories. Some mentors focus on your overall career trajectory. Others focus on a specific area of development, such as grant development, data plan management, or selecting journals for publication. Mentors should guide you in navigating the norms of the discipline and serve as a sounding board for your ideas and decisions. Of course, no single mentor should cover all these areas; it is important to identify mentors who will focus on a specific area of need. Trust between mentor and mentee is the cornerstone of this partnership, especially when mentoring across difference. For mentoring relationships that cross race and/or gender lines, it may help to identify mutual commonalities that may serve as an initial foundation for deepening this scholarly relationship. Mentors should consider how race and/or gender privilege grants them access to academic and other forms of capital that you may lack. They should be able to talk about harmful biases and stereotypes, and be willing to continue to enhance their cultural competency. It is a must that the mentors' understanding of how dominant norms and systems work to obstruct and invalidate women of color scholars will enable them to give credible, practical advice.

I have found that understanding what effective mentoring looks and feels like has made me a better judge of whom to invite into my Thrive Mosaic network. When I have identified someone who would be a good mentor in general (though not yet for my Mosaic), I meet with them to discuss my specific interest in their work and the areas in which I hope to be mentored. I provide them with my curriculum vita and biography, and other information I think would be helpful for them to know. If they agree to serve as my mentor, we clarify our meeting frequency, primary mode of communication, and other details of our mentor-mentee relationship. These clarifications sometimes require more exchanges than that initial conversation. I make sure I am prepared for our meetings, and I listen, listen, and listen some more. I share my progress on any action items.

For this new mentoring relationship to develop into a Mosaic relationship, I initiate conversations about mentoring across difference and gauge their willingness to increase their cross-cultural capacities. I have had experiences with mentors who are difficult to connect with or even get on their calendars. I have had mentors who seem disinterested, either in my work or in engaging in scholarly discourse. These are signs of a mentor who is lacking, either in skill or will, and you should decide the best way to disengage from that relationship.

Coach

A *coach* helps to facilitate thinking about your strengths and weaknesses, and can help you to move towards your goals. A coach, similar to an athletic coach, identifies your star qualities and helps that star shine brighter. Most executive or academic coaches today have some cross-cultural capacity, as the profession is moving in that direction. To promote them to the role of Thrive Mosaic coach, they should have a reasonable amount of expertise and skill in working across race and gender lines when working with you. When identifying a coach, you should reach out to your networks and ask about their experience with cross-cultural engagement.

A colleague recommended to me someone who fit my criteria for a Thrive Mosaic coach. Through conversations with my new coach, I learned that one of my weaknesses was communicating my progress, whether to a mentor, my department chair, or my Provost. I don't like to share my work until I feel that it is perfect. My coach helped me to think about how to "let go of my work"—article drafts, memos in progress, etc.—earlier in the writing process. One strategy was to clearly watermark each document as a "draft"; I would mark every page of text, the cover page, and in the email subject lines related to the document. This helped to lower my anxiety around being severely judged because others were aware that I was sharing with them a work in progress. My coach and I examined whether stereotype threat was making it difficult for me to let go of my drafts—that is, the fear that I would fulfill negative stereotypes about women of color. The coach aided me in developing habits that got me beyond what was a debilitating practice.

Several years ago while at MIT, I participated in an academic leadership development program that assigned me an executive coach. My coach had no cross-cultural engagement experience, but was eager to do her own homework and work with me. She grappled with her racial discomfort throughout our time together, though we had some great conversations about how race figures into the coaching process. We worked on how I could build and manage a senior leadership team. We identified my strengths, star power, and weaknesses. We considered the possible range of interpersonal dynamics when an African-American woman is team leader. We practiced scenarios related to persuasion, dealing with resistance, and building alliances within this larger cross-cultural context. While she would have been effective in any case, her insights into how gender and race factored into my leadership allowed her to consider additional motivations for habits I needed to change and leadership strategies that were sensitive to the impact of gender and race. My coach was able to evolve her practice to that of a Thrive Mosaic coach.

Targeted Training

Targeted training is a short-term learning episode, usually a workshop or seminar that focuses on building particular skills (e.g., budget management or trustee board operations) or your knowledge of a particular content area (e.g., the latest developments in universal design of learning technologies). The training is usually just-in-time learning and very specific in content. This is the only Mosaic role that is not relationship-based. Targeted training does not require cross-cultural experience (although it would be useful); however, I include it in the Thrive Mosaic as a specific growth opportunity to which women of color scholars may not get connected through their collegial and institutional interactions.

I have used targeted training to take advantage of a new opportunity or to boost my confidence before entering an unfamiliar work arena (for example, serving on a college president's cabinet). The training often provides a sufficient foundation that helps me to muster the courage to enter intimidating, unknown environments with (at least the appearance of) confidence and poise, as opposed to letting fear talk me out of an opportunity. Some years ago, I learned of an opportunity to participate in efforts to establish an endowed graduate fellowship and named professorship in honor of an important MIT African-American alum. I had no experience or even an understanding of fundraising. I decided to attend a three-day fundraising "boot camp" and was subsequently able to walk the walk and talk the talk with fundraising staff, and also make valuable contributions to establishing this highly sought after endowed gift. My contributions to that effort led to me being tapped for other opportunities. Had I not undergone this training,

I might have talked myself out of trying something that was initially so intimidating. The importance of this training cannot be understated, especially when transitioning to a new role or making preparations to advance our careers.

Crafting Your Thrive Mosaic

Most Thrive Mosaic roles (e.g., associate, coach, mentor, and advocate) involve relationship-building and an expectation of reasonable cultural competency skills for all involved. The Thrive Mosaic becomes a meaningful framework that I use to move ideas to credible and relevant action. It prompts my reflection on its roles and relationships. I can envision how my relationships and networks might support my taking that brave first, second, or even thousandth step into unknown territories. I use my Mosaic network to challenge the existing normative white masculinist value structure and to gain equitable access to professional opportunities.

I have tweaked the organization of my Mosaic database over the years but its implementation is quite simple. I use spreadsheet software, namely Microsoft Excel, because it allows any number of labeled pages in a single spreadsheet. I label each page in the spreadsheet with one of the Mosaic roles (associate, mentor, advocate, etc.). Then, I set up columns for the kinds of information I want to track for each contact. I also record all our interactions, how we met, dates of our last contact, any action items, and other potentially useful information. The easiest way to populate a new Mosaic is to review your current contacts and enter those who might eventually take on other Thrive roles as connectors. I have found through experience that connector is a good "entry-level" role. You may already have relationships that are ready to move immediately into an advocate or associate role. Once you populate your Mosaic with current relationships, identify those roles that will need to be cultivated.

Over the years, through my own experiences and working with faculty and academic leadership, I have learned that various combinations of Thrive Mosaic roles become more important to activate at different stages of your career.[1] At the Assistant Professor/Lecturer stages of your career, the mentor, advocate, and targeted training roles are most important to cultivate and activate. A variety of mentors, both at your institution and beyond, can help you to transition into your new academic life and can ensure that you are developing in those areas that you will need for tenure and promotion. Advocates will be important for writing promotion letters and providing opportunities that dovetail into your promotion requirements.

At the Associate Professor/Senior Lecturer stages of your career, the coach, connectors, mentors, and target training become more important. Coaches are helpful at this stage while you explore where your passions lie and what new scholarly directions you might explore. Connectors can plug you into the new networks related to your burgeoning interests, including interdisciplinary interests. Both targeted training and mentors are helpful in preparing you for leadership opportunities, both inside your institution and within your disciplinary societies.

Finally, mentors, targeted training, coaches, and connectors are crucial when moving into academic leadership roles. In particular, you will look for mentors who can help with your transition from the faculty/lecturer arena and adjust to a very different way of relating to your institution and campus community. Connectors can bring you into academic leadership networks—for example, colleagues in similar roles at other institutions, consortia, and other kinds of academic leadership groups.

A robust Thrive Mosaic is broad and diverse and you should work to include people outside of your usual networks and your comfort zone. In particular, reach out across race, gender, other identities, as well as across disciplines and institutions. Your goal is always to re-access your connectors to determine which relationships may be ready to advance to mentor, advocate, or associate.

Activating Your Thrive Mosaic

To activate your Mosaic network, I recommend starting with a specific goal you wish to accomplish—let's say a grant proposal that you want to prepare. Start by contacting people in your Mosaic network who can address your questions or concerns. Personally, I always start by contacting a few associates to set up an accountability schedule to ensure steady progress on my grant writing. Next, I contact mentors who can advise me on preparing the various sections of the proposal or offer tips on how to increase my chances for funding. I might contact another mentor who can give me advice for handling a conversation with the program officer and the kinds of questions to expect. I find that "cold-calling" the program officer can be terrifying; it helps to have advanced understanding of how to facilitate a productive conversation. Additionally, I seek out targeted training by attending a workshop on how to prepare a successful grant proposal. Finally, I contact a number of advocates to request letters of support for the grant. The Thrive Mosaic makes this process systematic and strategic.

My Thrive Mosaic has been invaluable for combating discrimination, particularly when there was a power differential between the more powerful aggressor and myself. Let me provide an example. As a graduate student, I cultivated a mentor-mentee relationship with a white male professor in my department. He held a high-level senior leadership position at MIT and has been a vocal advocate for underrepresented students. He and I would discuss issues of race in the academy and other social justice topics. I decided to make him a part of my Thrive Mosaic, and he accepted my invitation to join. Meanwhile, my lab moved to another building where everyone, except for another Black student and me, was assigned office space. Our repeated inquires to the lab director were countered with "be patient while other space issues were resolved." Mind you, every person in the lab had been assigned office space and the only remaining issues involved where to house equipment. After a week of using Barker Library as an office, I decided I had enough, but I was afraid to push the lab director for fear of retaliation. I explained the situation to my new Thrive mentor who was able to have a conversation with the lab director about "the strange lack of space for all our graduate students." My mentor was able to settle the issue without me being involved directly; the other student and I had offices later that day. My Thrive mentor was able to intervene on my behalf in a way that shielded me from any negative fallout. What is perhaps most important was that I did not have to explain to my Thrive mentor why the behavior was discriminatory or convince him to intervene on my behalf.

Fiery Intellect, Full Heart, Brave Soul

The Thrive Mosaic is my instrument for scholar-activism. My intention in wielding this instrument is to disrupt the academy in ways that support African-American women's full participation as scholars, teachers, innovators, and whatever else we choose to be. As Black women, we will not have true freedom as long as our participation in the academy requires us to compromise ourselves or our history. This insight is illustrated by the African proverb, "If you cut your chains, you free yourself. If you cut your roots, you die." If we are to remain whole while bringing the full value of our scholarship to bear, then we must maintain our roots.

The Mosaic Thrive is my tool for advancing my work of social justice and supporting my risk-taking, and leveraging Thrive Mosaic relationships to fuel my resilience and optimism. In these ways, I am able to navigate HWCUs and get to where I need to be in spite of racist and sexist structures and behaviors, and without rejecting my true self. Implicit in the Thrive Mosaic is the notion that we all need multiple mentors, multiple advocates, multiple connectors, etc. to cover all the areas of growth over time. At different stages of my career or for specific aspirations, I will focus on activating the affordances of particular roles within my network. I am more productive in my writing and teaching because of my associates and mentors. I enjoy opportunities because of my advocates and, in many cases, gain opportunities previously unknown to me. I have been able to face and overcome fear by engaging my Mosaic to gain deeper insight into complex situations, knowledge to navigate challenges successfully, and strengthen practices of resiliency. My Mosaic relationships provide the care and knowledge necessary to journey from graduate student to lecturer to senior administrator, and walk the path I choose to follow. Many prestigious or formative opportunities have come my way through this incredible network.

As African-American women scholars, I hope you will consider being an associate, mentor, advocate, etc. to other women of color scholars and professionals. When we increase our numbers, we create a stronger network of women scholars and strengthen the supports we deserve in our careers. Looking back, I doubt I would have persisted on my journey to a PhD without my Thrive Mosaic advocates, mentors, associates, connectors, etc. In those moments when I think to abandon the academy because of yet another sexist or racist obstacle, my Thrive Mosaic network bolsters my resilience and works to minimize the threat. This network encourages me to bring my whole self, including my race and gender, to the realization of my goals, my future, and my life. My commitment to social justice in academia for myself and other African-American women scholars thrives because of a special network that is personally and culturally relevant, and cognizant of the significance of my race and my gender to my journey.

Acknowledgments

For my nephew, Brandon, I remain brave so you will know bravery as your legacy.

Note

1 For information about how to leverage the Thrive Mosaic in support of the various stages of your career, see Chapman (2016, Feb.11).

Reference

Chapman, R. (2016, February 11). *THRIVE Mosaic: The six strategic influences every academic should cultivate for career growth and success* [Webinar]. In Higher Education Recruitment Consortium (HERC) Webinars. Retrieved from https://vimeo.com/155026394

12 Courageous Xicanas

Living Legacies of *Comadrazgo* in the Academy

Kandace Creel Falcón

A colleague stopped me in the hall as I walked from my classroom back to my office. She said, "Kandace you are so brave." Confused, I paused before responding to see whether there was more to her statement. She continued, "I just could never wear my hair like that, and especially before tenure." I laughed, she stared blankly. I guess she was serious. In 2012, desperate for a style change, I chose a bold undercut look with hot pink highlights. Since then, I'd grown accustomed to strange looks whenever I walked into crowded restaurants occupied by mostly cisgender, heterosexual, and white patrons in my West Central Minnesota small-town life. I also gave up trying to discern exactly which piece of my identity contributed most to the hush that fell over the crowd when I walked into a space as a queer femme Xicana, flamboyantly announcing myself visually. These same identities announce me as different in most spaces I navigate, both on and off campus.

It certainly takes confidence to rock this look in Fargo, North Dakota, but I wouldn't exactly say that it's a *courageous* act. When white women compliment my hair, they often frame it in terms of how they "could never." Black women, however, legitimately compliment my hair with appreciation of the color and the shape, rarely positioning themselves in relation to my hair. Once, while packing up at a conference following the delivery of a paper, a Latina graduate student found me in the crowd and asked, "do you get any kind of pushback from your students or administrators about your hair?" I chuckled, "I think my hair is the least of my concerns." Sometimes I wish my hair was the bravest thing about me, but as a Xicana in the academy, I know that my very presence in the university is a testament to our courageous legacies.

Courage Is Action Rooted in Xicana Legacy

In the Introduction of *[Un]framing the Bad Woman: Sor Juana, Malinche, Coyolxauhqui and Other Rebels with a Cause*, Alicia Gaspar de Alba (2014) writes of the methodology that ties together her Xicana feminist text: "I found that what the women I write about have in common, and the reason they interest me in the first place, is that they are all rebels with a cause, and I see myself represented in their mirror" (5). To be a Xicana feminist is to embody this sense of a rebel with a cause; we see ourselves in the mirror of the actions women take and the confines of society that spur their actions. Our presence in academia relies not only on our strength and courage to demand a place there, but it is rooted in our resistant pasts. When you need reminders of your rebel spirit, hone in on that feeling of knowing that someone has your back. Xicana theorists have long characterized the relationship between us and our white feminist sisters as the bridge we call our backs (Moraga & Anzaldúa, 1981). This "bridge" can represent the negative signifier of the erasure of the contributions of women of color to feminist movements; or even worse, the way white feminism takes from women of color feminism without attribution and through appropriation. For Xicanas used to being trampled in this sense, building networks through purposeful mentorship allows us to both "get our backs up" and have each other's backs when times get tough.

I learned the value of this purposeful mentorship young while interning at the Albuquerque Rape Crisis Center, reporting to a young Xicana femme feminist. And I was reminded again of the importance of mentorship when I chose to pursue my PhD at the University of Minnesota working with my Xicana doctoral advisor in the Gender, Women's and Sexuality Studies Department, Dr. Edén E. Torres. As Xicana scholar-activists in the academy, we learn from our mentors much more than how to successfully complete a dissertation. The Xicanas who mentor new or younger Xicana scholar-activists do so as a vital legacy of generational mentorship. These women carry within them the legacy of our feminist foremothers, who confronted institutional powers in their day. Those who challenged the confines of patriarchy *and* other forces serve to inspire us. They include mujeres like La Malintzín, a reclaimed Indigenous ambassador who prevented wars during Spanish colonization in the 16th century of current Mexico, Sor Juana Ines de la Cruz, a devout nun who challenged the Catholic Church in 17th-century Mexico, and the unnamed soldaderas of the Mexican Revolution, women who took up arms to support radical change in 20th-century Mexico. Other heroes of the 20th century include women like Frida Kahlo (a communist artist who critiqued capitalism and made art as a form of resistance globally) and Emma Tenayuca (a Mexican-American union organizer who led strikes on behalf of exploited women laborers in pecan shelling factories). These women remind us of our strength and resilience and our ability to embody courage in contentious spaces. Perhaps, because we are not meant for these academic halls, our tongues are not so tightly bound.

Apart from mentoring Xicana/o graduate and undergraduate students, my mentor Edén Torres is a force on her campus. As my advisor, she routinely regaled me and other students of color with vivid tales of her resistance when she was not taken seriously: as a student, junior faculty member, or department chair. Those are her stories to tell, but it is through my observations of Edén, and other Xicana scholar-activists who speak out against injustices on their campuses, that I have the courage to hit the *send* button on emails promoting campus organizing in the face of what often feels like minimal administrative support. Edén's leadership and guidance inspire me when organizing a direct response is necessary. Because Xicana feminism emerges out of contestation, to be silent, passive, or complicit in acts of injustice directly contradicts my Xicana feminist investments.

Courage Is Knowing Your Truth

On September 3, 2014, my university administration sent a campus-wide email with the subject "Students take action for safety of fellow student," informing us of a vague campus safety "incident" that took place in a residence hall earlier. Scrolling Facebook the next day, I came upon a local broadcast news report titled, "MSUM Student Accused of Rape in Dorm Room, Asking Other Students to Watch." Because the video and accompanying article mentioned that the alleged crime happened in a MSUM residence hall, I slowly began to draw connections between the previous day's quickly deleted email and this story in my social media feed. To say that I experienced dismay would be an understatement. My body and spirit filled with the anger, rage, sorrow, and the deep sense of injustice that I had come to know too often from my ten years working in higher education institutional spaces. Sorrow soon overtook the other feelings; I felt defeated. This frustration piled on top of the previous student disclosures to which I bore witness. Because I am a professor of Women's and Gender Studies, many students share their experiences of sexual violence with me following classroom discussions. As a queer Xicana feminist on campus, students seek me out as a trusted faculty member to lay bare a variety of experiences of injustice, even when not enrolled in my class. With each telling, I carry with me the lived realities ranging from racial discrimination to occurrences of homophobia, transphobia, and gender-based violence from students who seek comfort and guidance in how to cope with what they endure. Sometimes they share their stories to seek accountability for the injustices they withstand in our institutional space. Other times, they just need a compassionate ear.

Perhaps I would not have been filled with such dismay if not for the other institutional challenges in which I simultaneously attempted to intervene. Earlier in 2014, the university launched a First Year Experience (FYE) course mandatory for all incoming first-year students. The faculty worked to develop a shared curriculum, and healthy decision-making regarding sexual activity and alcohol was one of the mandatory weekly course sessions. At one point over the summer, a colleague shared an inflammatory article—grounded in blaming women for their own sexual assault because of drinking—as discussion material for the course. Appalled by the "resource," with my blood pressure rising, I immediately began working with Alison, the Director of the Faculty Development Center, to develop a future faculty training for my colleagues.

When I showed up to the Faculty Development Center to start the first 8:15 am scheduled faculty training session, the university President and Interim Provost were seated at the table with notebooks open. The sessions had been planned long before this recent sexual assault on campus but were particularly well attended because of the organizing I did in light of the news of the "incident." With the President's presence, the stakes were high. As facilitator, I chose to go on with the program as planned. I mentioned the history of the lack of feminist resources highlighted in the online learning platform for professors to consult. I discussed the conversations in which Alison and I engaged over several months on how to make the most of training time with faculty to better prepare them for their classes. The President peered up from her open notebook with a confused look on her face—a pensive, bordering on scowl, look. She asked, "So, this isn't just about what happened this week?" I replied, "No. It's just an unfortunate coincidence that we have such a clear example to unpack this week as to what our campus response looks like when sexual violence happens here."

I read their presence at the session as their defensive effort to make sure that administration was present to provide their point of view. Reflecting on this event years later, I still remember the feelings in my body. I felt fueled by the adrenaline high I get when I know my stuff and I'm in front of a crowd. I felt a lot riding on my performance, which had the opportunity to impact many more beyond the room of twelve faculty and two administrators. I felt fear, too. I stepped into my leadership role untenured and in the first month of my first semester as the Director of our Women's and Gender Studies program, looking for ways to hold an institution accountable to the burdens, pains, and traumas queer and trans people of color faculty and students carry with us in this space.

I know that to do this work is not without risk—risk of being seen as "confrontational," "aggressive," or "fiery" because of the implicit biases those of the dominant group might hold of Xicanas/Latinas. There may be other risks within the academy including not earning tenure, marginalization within one's own department, and being framed by your colleagues as "adversarial." The Dean has called me into his office to patronizingly lecture me on the risks of my written "tone" being misunderstood by other administrators. Another administrator once asked me for a meeting to discuss what I tweet on Twitter. Despite this constant low-level surveillance of my actions within the academy, I am inspired by the daily and cumulative acts of bravery Xicanas enact in university spaces in spite of real risks. I am privileged in the sense that I have no children to feed, no real ties to this community that put additional constraints on my actions beyond the rules set by the academy. This helps me to feel a little better when facing a wall of apathy from colleagues beleaguered by the powers that be, resigned that nothing will ever change. On days when I struggle, I spend a lot of time thinking about how we keep going, what keeps some of us moving forward despite the burdens of institutional injustices. I wonder: how do our Xicana feminist frames allow us to simultaneously see injustice *and* demand better of our institutions?

I answer this question by honoring historical figures and modeling the actions of my mentors' might as a source of our Xicana feminist fires. Xicana rebels also enact the Xicana feminist concept of *comadrazgo* as a frame for understanding Xicana scholar-activist work in predominately white Midwestern educational spaces. In Xicana feminism, *comadrazgo* represents alternative formations of kinship that characterize a deep support of other women. It grows out of the Mexican Catholic practice of mothers building relationships with other women, *comadres*, who help support the care and development of each other's children. As historian Vicki Ruiz (2008) notes of the experiences of Mexican migrant farmworkers in the US, "*Commadrazgo* (sic) served as one of the undergirdings for general patterns of reciprocity as women cared for one another as family and neighbors" (p. 16). Rosa Linda Fregoso (2003) theorizes *comadrazgo* as a means to read against the so-called natural, patriarchal nationalist Chicano family formation. Both Keta Miranda (2003) and Maylei Blackwell (2011) theorize *comadrazgo* as politicized networks of women's solidarity in their studies on Xicana gang members and on Xicana student-activists, respectively.

I use the frame of *comadrazgo* to account for the political networks of support and kinship we build as Xicanas in the academy to sustain one another so as to enable us to keep our rebel spirits strong within the realm of oppressive academic institutions. We are *comadres* to each other when we help birth dissertations and books and scholarship that impact lives beyond small circles of academics. We are also *comadres* when we lift each other up from our institutional spaces because we intimately know what it is like to be the only one.

Courage Is Paving the Way for Others

As the only full-time faculty member in Women's and Gender Studies, I often feel alone on my campus as a politicized, purposefully intersectional, Xicana femme feminist. Yet, I am not alone when I have the chance to reconnect with my *comadres* in other institutional settings at conferences, online, or through our scholarship. I am also privileged to be a scholar-activist in Women's and Gender Studies, as our disciplinary space also shields me from (some of) the backlash that we face in the academy when we demand better of university institutions.

Because our discipline is grounded by the politics of activism and theory coming together in the space of the academy, institutions housing Women's and Gender Studies programs or departments at some level tolerate our existence and know what they are in for with our presence. Our presence in these hallowed halls enables administrators to admit that, in addition to helping them meet their diversity and inclusion goals on paper, we also serve to enact their diversity and inclusion goals in practice. I embrace diversity and inclusion goal language in university documents as my mandate for speaking up, for speaking out, for calling out, and for calling in. This is how I came out of my place of dismay to organizing direct responses to institutionalized sexism and the perpetuation of gender-based violence on my campus. I was enabled by the training and rich history of brave Xicanas and privileged to be in a discipline that expects us all to directly challenge to systems of oppression. Xicana rebels support one another by repaying the debts of the foremothers who supported us, linking Xicana feminist activism across generations by making larger paths for those who come behind us.

It is difficult to reflect on bravery, especially in our Minnesota Midwestern culture, because to speak too much or too highly about oneself is to brag and be boastful. I write this story as an attempt to capture, make sense of, and amplify Xicana feminism as one who lives "without apology" (Torres, 2003), like my mentor taught me. I write to reflect on how saying something publicly and organizing larger campus responses to abuse become radical acts in the face of complicit acceptance of the status quo. Sending an email may not seem so brave until you understand the inherent risks to rocking the boat. Those emails resulted in my colleagues expressing fear that the university administration would retaliate against me. Have you ever spent the whole day with your university president as a result of a couple of emails and session planning on campus? At the time, I did not know what would be the outcome of organizing; all that I knew was that I could not quietly allow what transpired in terms of communication to our larger campus community regarding gendered violence.

While externally, some may see my hot pink highlighted hair as the main expression of my courageous sensibilities, I've never thought about my hair as the sole sense of how I embody acts of bravery in the academy. True acts of courage involve bringing together scholarship and direct action organizing for collectively determined campus change. True acts of courage mean sharing these stories, acknowledging my role and the roles of others that resulted in the formation of a Sexual Violence Prevention Committee on campus with formal goals and measures to try to prevent this from happening again. True acts of courage are exemplified by those who fight for the continued presence of Women's and Gender Studies on campus *and* those who do intersectional feminist work that develops scholar-activists within and beyond the academy. True acts of courage carry on our *comadrazgo* traditions linking our efforts of today to those who come before and those who will come long after we are gone.

Acknowledgments

I thank Alexandra Mendoza Covarrubias for suggesting the frame of *comadrazgo* for better understanding Xicana academic bravery. An earlier version of this chapter was presented at the 16th Annual Red River

Women's Studies Conference held in October 2016 in Grand Forks, North Dakota. I am grateful for the editorial and technical assistance of Kynsey M. Creel and Nathan Tylutki in the preparations of this manuscript.

References

Blackwell, M. (2011). *¡Chicana power! Contested histories of feminism in the Chicano movement*. Austin, TX: University of Texas Press.

Fregoso, R. L. (2003). *MeXicana encounters: The making of social identities on the borderlands*. Berkeley, CA: University of California Press.

Gaspar de Alba, A. (2014). *[Un]Framing the "bad woman": Sor Juana, Malinche, Coyolxauhqui and other rebels with a cause*. Austin, TX: University of Texas Press.

Miranda, M. K. (2003). *Homegirls in the public sphere*. Austin, TX: University of Texas Press.

Moraga, C., & Anzaldúa, G. (1981). *This bridge called my back: Writings by radical women of color* (1st ed.). Watertown, MA: Persephone Press.

Ruiz, V. (2008). *From out of the shadows: Mexican women in twentieth-century America, 10th anniversary edition*. New York, NY and Oxford: Oxford University Press.

Torres, E. E. (2003). *Chicana without apology: The new Chicana cultural studies*. New York, NY: Routledge.

13 "We Got You"

What Raising Up the Next Generation of Scholar-Activists Has Taught Me

Janelle M. Silva

This essay maps how my scholar-activist identity has emerged at my current institution and the brave acts that I have taken to collaborate with students of color to achieve their goal of equity and inclusion on our campus. By centering the discussion on how teaching can be an activist effort, I explore how I often risk my own career to ensure the well-being of my students. As I reflect on my activism, I will also address the strategies that I have employed to minimize any backlash from my institution and how I have attempted to maintain balance between activism and my personal life. For the reader, I hope that my brave actions and the risks that I have navigated can be a catalyst for your own bravery.[1]

Teaching as an Activist Effort: Brave Acts from the Classroom

Teaching has always been an activist effort for me. As a woman of color, I strongly believe that my presence in the college classroom is a form of activism, especially in environments where the number of faculty of color is small. Drawing upon bell hooks (2010, 2003, 1994), I view my classroom as a community, wherein we engage in critical dialog centered around difference, power, and privilege, as we work toward solutions for collective action. As a social-community psychologist, I strive to facilitate moments of action for students, bridging classroom and subject knowledge that is connected to their lives. Students who enroll in my classes are well aware that I use class projects as catalysts for improving our campus by building on the skills that they have acquired in their respective majors. Ideally, it is my goal that students enter my classroom acknowledging John Brown Childs's (2003) sentiment that "we all live in different rooms," but together we "must learn how to live in that house as *one*." Through my teaching, I instill in my students a sense of the importance of recognizing difference and understanding how power and social structures shape a person's lived experiences, as well as how to use the skills they have acquired to work toward social change.

I realize that one of the greatest resources with which I can provide my students is the ability to use my classroom as a space for transformative learning and action. Over the past six years, I have facilitated activist moments in my classes through class projects and student mentorship. My students have engaged in various forms of activism, including a campus-wide survey and assessment regarding the need for a campus Women's Center (Silva & the Students for Gender Equity, 2015), promoting the concept of a Wellness & Health Center, and amplifying the voices of student-activists through qualitative research. As each of these efforts has facilitated change on our campus, they have also presented various risks for both my students and me as their professor. The most visible and riskiest form of student activism that emerged from my classroom was the student walkout for a campus Diversity Center that originated in my Institutions & Social Change course.

The Institutions & Social Change course introduced students to how others have identified points of contention within institutions and facilitated social change. I committed to providing students with an opportunity to embody the writings of social activists, theorists, and scholars through their own social change. This commitment was driven largely by the needs of our campus community. I had recently changed the final project from small group research projects to one class wide project that required the students to identify a social institution and facilitate some form of action. Called the Practical Activism Project, the project instructed students to work as a collective, conduct research, integrate course material, and perform an action. I viewed this project as an opportunity to understand their frustrations in regard to campus politics, society, and their greater community by applying theory into action.

When the students in my winter 2015 Institutions & Social Change class met to determine the focus of their Practical Activism Project, many discussed how they wanted to use the assignment as an opportunity to draw attention to the need for a Diversity Center on campus. Their desire for a campus Diversity Center was not a surprise to me. Among four-year universities in Washington state, the University of Washington, Bothell, has the most diverse student body, yet lacks spaces on campus to adequately meet these students' needs. Students' frustrations about not having a campus Diversity Center had reached a boiling point. Campus town halls and Chancellor Forums left many students frustrated and with more questions than answers. As a class, the students spent two weeks investigating the university, learning about the past tensions over developing such a center on campus, and discussing why these spaces are critical for students. Drawing upon the works of Martin Luther King Jr., Earl Babbie, and Saul Alinsky, they collectively decided that they would have a campus walkout. On February 25, 2015, 45 undergraduate students from my Institutions & Social Change course led a campus-wide walkout for a Diversity Center at UW Bothell.

The night before the walkout, I couldn't sleep. I was scared that no one would actually walk out. I was nervous that faculty would not support the students' action. My stomach was twisted in knots with the fear that I may have led them to failure and humiliation. I logged onto Facebook at midnight, posting a message about the walkout, the purpose, and encouraging my colleagues to join us. At noon, I could hear students walking out of classrooms. As I made my way down the stairs to the public square, I could see a crowd growing from 50 to over 400 students, faculty, and staff. Standing in the rain, students spoke out about their isolation on campus. They shared what it meant to be students who are undocumented, veterans, single mothers, transgender, queer, Muslim, and Latinx on a campus that had no Diversity Center.

I stood there with my colleagues, listening intently to each student speak, watching the campus administration weave through the crowd. When the students asked me to speak, my hands shook as I took the megaphone. I had nothing prepared as I did not know that they planned for me to speak at the walkout. I decided to follow their lead and speak from the heart. I spoke directly to the students, telling them that I see them and hear them, and reaffirming that what they were demanding—a Diversity Center—should be given. I only know what I said because of the video footage that the students' took as part of their Practical Activism Project. After I spoke, I returned to the crowd to join others as the students began their march. We marched through the main academic building that housed campus administration, staging a sit-in in the Chancellor's Office, giving him a list of demands, and explaining their actions. In response to their efforts and those of their peers, past and present, our institution developed a five-year campus Diversity Action Plan with a commitment to a temporary Diversity Center to be open in spring 2017. This meant that the students' demand for a campus Diversity Center would become a reality.

Risks: Strategies for Negotiating Tensions

The opening of the temporary Diversity Center has been one of my most rewarding teacher moments. However, with these rewards also come risks. By creating transformative classroom environments, I was aware that doing projects that could lead to student activism was risky, especially if this activism challenged the institution itself. As I made my way back to my office after the walkout, a few of my colleagues stopped me to ask whether the students leading the walkout were in my class. When I said yes, some walked away, while others reassured me that I should still be fine for tenure and that I should send some emails "to apologize to upper administration . . . in case [I] was worried." That evening, I received a few emails from faculty and staff suggesting that I should "be careful" and even questioning my pedagogy. My unwavering support for students of color on our campus was not new, but my collaboration with them on their activism was now highly visible through the walkout.

Although my students often engage in activism in my class projects, this was the first one that directly challenged the institution. As a junior faculty member woman of color, I knew that I was putting myself at risk, both personally and professionally. I was asking students to hold their institution accountable to its mission of diversity and social justice. There was a risk in how the administration might interpret my pedagogy. There was also the risk that some students may have enrolled in my courses to complete a degree requirement, without any interest in facilitating social change. I was concerned that these students might take their frustrations out by criticizing me in course evaluations or complaining to my dean about my teaching. When I presented the 45-person project on the first day of class, students responded with smiles, confusion, uncertainty, annoyance, and disbelief. "Professor Silva, can you repeat yourself please?" was a common phrase I heard from students. They thought I meant 4-person small group projects, not the entire class of 45 students. I knew students would attempt to "get out" of the project, but I stood my ground. In knowing to anticipate these risks, I took some precautions ahead of the walkout.

Although all of my courses are known to emphasize collective action and social change, I needed to be sure that the connection between activism and the curricula was visible to my students, colleagues, and university administration. One strategy that I employed to counteract critiques of my approach was through developing carefully crafted, transparent course syllabi. I took great lengths to create projects that—to an outsider's perspective—were "academically valid" in both rigor and assessment. I restructured syllabi and lectures to make visible why each project was an important component of student learning. Smaller assignments were created to build onto the larger class assignment (a teaching practice called "scaffolding"). I assigned readings that complemented the concept of social action and offered students critiques of what activism means, especially for privileged students. I wanted the idea of activism to follow the course narrative and not be viewed as merely moments to agitate or disrupt campus activities. In addition, to gain student buy-in in projects like practical activism, I stepped back and allowed *them* to lead, determining the action. Trust—what some might consider "blind" trust—was central to this process. I had to trust them and believe that they would not put my job or their education at risk. This meant trusting students whom I did not know very well and believing that they were taking the necessary precautions (i.e., university rules, code of conduct) before engaging in any action-based work. In turn, they had to trust that I would support their action and defend them if needed.

I also had to consider the potential risks of my approach to teaching outside of the classroom. My class projects heightened my visibility on campus and presented additional risks in terms of colleagues' perceptions of me. Although I did have some privilege as an assistant professor, I was still vulnerable because I was not yet tenured. Each time a colleague would comment how much they "admired [my] bravery," "you just don't seem to care what they [administration] thinks," or "I wouldn't have done that before tenure," I was reminded of my vulnerable status within the institution. I was concerned about what risks I had taken in doing this work. Some might argue that the "smart" or "safe" approach would have been to wait until I earned tenure to use my classes for community action projects. Yet, each time that I witnessed students confront university administration, I was deeply aware of the public display of their vulnerability. Many students were not afraid to announce their marginalized statuses as queer, undocumented, transgender, disabled, etc. As brave as the students were, they, too, were concerned about how the campus community interpreted their actions.

To mitigate these additional risks, I maintain clear and open communication with my dean and mentors about what is going on in my classes. My dean and senior colleagues have been supportive of the relationships that I have cultivated with students and how I have integrated our work into student-centered scholarship. I am fortunate that I feel valued, respected, and heard by my dean and mentors. I do not take this for granted, as I know many women of color faculty members who do not have the same trust. Maintaining strong communication with my department has been critical to my ability to use my position to amplify students' needs. I have the privilege of having multiple mentors who will speak honestly and openly to me about the risks in which I am placing myself and who are willing to develop strategies on how to minimize these risks. I strongly believe in the value of identifying allies within one's department or institution who have seniority and will defend one if challenged. Although my mentors caution me on certain actions, they also have allowed me to step into roles others might believe are not appropriate for a junior faculty member because they believe in me. Through their mentorship and support, I believe I have been able to change the view of me as a "troublemaker" to a campus asset.

Besides mentors and supportive administrators, I also reached out to other faculty whom I felt would be empathetic and had more institutional leverage on campus than myself. Tenured faculty often face fewer risks for speaking out than pre-tenured faculty of color. Many of these colleagues offered their support; they were aware of the risks in which I was placing myself by speaking out and often being the only one at the table. The intention was not to remove myself from these conversations, but to create a coalition of faculty invested in these students' needs from all ranks. Reaching out was a strategic move beyond developing a cohesive faculty voice. It allowed me to inform other faculty of the work that I was doing, knowing that these people would be voting on my promotion. I was both protecting myself, as well as my students.

An additional strategy that I utilized was to increase visibility of student activism. Rather than relying on the institution to write our history, my students and I captured it through our scholarship. I have mentored students who have won prestigious university fellowships and awards where we have written manuscripts (to submit for publication) on decolonizing the university through the process of student activism. Our writing has served two purposes: it is a cathartic time for us to process our activism and emotions, while further legitimizing this work as scholarship and academically valid. I have also gained visibility of our activism through campus partnerships. My partnerships with our student newspaper and campus library have ensured that our voices were central to the documentation of student activism. Institutional memory is often lost once students leave. Many of our student-activists have a difficult time leaving the institution for fear that their work will stop. I work with our student-activists to keep a record of their work. Campus libraries can help archive student activism on campus and can be a great resource to maintain this history. Many colleagues expressed concern about the risks inherent in the visibility that comes with being present, joining students, and using our voices. Students know that I will protect them as much as I can in my position. However, in order to continue to protect them, I must also protect myself.

For me, as for many women of color faculty, these risks will always be present. Even when there are allies or ways to mitigate backlash, the risks do not vanish. The difference for me in this moment is my ability to manage these risks as I continue to be brave.

Balance: Professional and Personal

Given my teaching and support for student-activists, it did not take long for me to gain a reputation among the students as "one to connect with." My activist teaching led me to be placed on high-profile campus committees, invitations to speak at campus forums on diversity, and opportunities to facilitate discussions and workshops on pedagogy. The more I connected with students, the more colleagues cautioned me that being one of six Latinx faculty and being present could affect my work-life balance. It is a risk of personal time and professional development. For tenure-track faculty, the "tenure clock" is constantly ticking. I was strongly encouraged by colleagues to avoid doing anything that would not count towards tenure. It would have been much simpler for me focus my energy on my research. I remember sitting in meetings with other junior faculty, envious of how relaxed they appeared. Although we were all building new projects, I often felt that I was carrying the additional unpaid labor that so many junior faculty of color—women of color in particular—take on given our commitments to our communities. I found it difficult to share my struggles with finding both work-life balance and work-research-student balance with colleagues whose experiences vastly differed from my own.

Unbeknownst to me, my activist teaching and support for student-activists would lead me to a much deeper, emotional risk. Through listening and building community with students, I started to "take on" their pain. I felt their tears and anger deeply. This extended beyond school, as students started to share with me their personal struggles and leaned on me for advice. My office became a part-time workspace, full-time therapy space. I struggled with "leaving work at work"; I thought about them all of the time. I often found myself staying up late at night searching for community resources that they could utilize, including therapists, support groups, and safe homes. I knew that I could not save them and it was never my intention to do so. I just wanted to ease some of their burden and use my skills to help locate other places of support. It became common for me to spend my time completing lectures, grading, typing up field notes, and answering my students' emails. At times, I felt lost within this struggle. I struggled with what these boundaries should look like, given how much these students needed allies on multiple levels. My bravery was beginning to take a toll on my own physical and mental health.

I knew that if I was going to be a successful collaborator with these students, I could not "fall apart." This was not limited to my professional well-being, but also included my physical and mental health. I was well aware of the daily struggle student-activists faced in wanting to do it all at the risk of their own well-being. As their mentor, I wanted to model for my students the importance of taking care of themselves. During weekly meetings with one another in my office, I was honest with the students about being tired and exhausted, often forgetting to eat lunch because of work, or how I had not seen the latest movie because I did not make time for a social life. I trusted that the students would not share our private conversations with others, just as they trusted I would not share the things they said with me.

It was not my intention to put my worries or concerns on these students, but to show them that faculty are humans, too. Naively, the students often mentioned how faculty must have it "all together" given our academic positions. I wanted them to know we struggle with balance just like them; I took the risk of sharing my struggles in order to talk to them about how I was going to attempt to alleviate these risks. I started to keep healthy snacks in my office for all of us to eat. I shared my personal calendar with them so that they could see how I blocked out time for running—my physical stress reliever. Collectively, we established boundaries for work, agreeing not to send emails or discuss action plans between 5pm on Friday evening and 9am on Monday morning, and that no work should take place on holidays. Small steps towards work-life balance gave us great rewards in terms of energy, mood, demeanor, and focus.

It would feel disingenuous of me to discuss balance if I ignored how my involvement on campus impacts my personal life at home. As we moved forward with creating a temporary Diversity Center on campus, I took on the role as the faculty advocate of student activism and its importance in this project. Again, this role meant greater commitments, additional meetings, longer hours spent on campus, and heightened visibility—all while still producing scholarly work, maintaining an active research agenda, and teaching. My mentors warned me of the risks in terms of my professional commitments and the impact to my personal life. As I was recently married, colleagues did not want me to sacrifice my marriage for this work. I made sure to make these decisions with my partner and to honor our time at home together. Right now, my partner and I have to balance our individual careers with household work and taking care of our pets. If we had children, the balancing act would be even more difficult and necessary. I know that I am not perfect when it comes to centering my marriage over this work. This is something that I work on every day. Some days I succeed, and some days I fail. I talk to my students about the importance of balancing their personal lives with their activism. I tell them that they should do the same, since I was well aware of how often activists—especially women activists— sacrifice their personal life for this work. This is a part of our honoring one another as whole people.

"Remember, We Got You": A Final Thought

It seems somewhat fitting that I wrote this essay just as I prepared to turn in my tenure file. The tenure process remains an unclear and mysterious one to my students, but they are aware that tenure can make acts of bravery less risky. A few days ago, at the time of writing this essay, an alum and a current student—both womxn of color—came by my office for an impromptu visit. They were both activists who have transformed our institution in tremendous ways. We talked about their families, classes, jobs, internships, graduate school, study abroad, and the ongoing work towards the campus Diversity Center. As we laughed and shared our lives, they paused.

STUDENT: "Dr. Silva, how's your tenure stuff going?"
ME: "It's going."
ALUM: "When is it due?"
ME: "I have to turn my packet in this spring."
ALUM: "Are you nervous?"
ME: "Well, I think we all get a bit nervous about the unknown."
    The alum and student look at one another and then turn to me.
ALUM (SMILING): "Don't worry about this, Dr. Silva, you got this."
STUDENT: "Yeah, and we will stage a sit-in in your office if you don't. Remember, you got us and we got you."

My students have taught me to be brave. In times when I have feared losing my job because of my activism on campus or potential student punishment for speaking out, I have known that we have each other's back. I frequently choose to be brave and take risks because of the pride my students have when they realize what they have done to push our institution forward and hold it accountable to its mission of serving its diverse student body. I am fortunate to have played a small role in that dialog and that student-activists on campus know that they can come to me for support, despite never having me as a professor. That makes being brave worth the risks.

Acknowledgments

The author would like to thank her students who continue to be the social justice warriors on our campus. She would also like to thank Mira Shima-bukuro for her reflections on this chapter, as well as Christian Anderson for being a sounding board for this project.

Note

1 The author would like to thank her students who continue to be the social justice warriors on our campus. She would also like to thank Mira Shimabukuro for her reflections on this chapter, as well as Christian Anderson for being a sounding board for this project.

References

Childs, J. B. (2003). *Transcommunality: From the politics of conversion to the ethics of respect*. Philadelphia: Temple University Press.

hooks, b. (1994). *Teaching to transgress: Education as the practice of freedom*. New York, NY and London: Routledge.

hooks, b. (2003). *Teaching community: A pedagogy of hope*. New York, NY and London: Routledge.

hooks, b. (2010). *Teaching critical thinking: Practical wisdom*. New York, NY and London: Routledge.

Silva, J. M., & the Students for Gender Equity. (2015). A feminist approach to teaching community psychology: The senior seminar project. *The Feminist Teacher*, *25*(2–3), 111–123.

14 On the Wings of Communal Bravery

Nelli Sargsyan

What does academic bravery look like at the intersection of many *homes*? In this autoethnographic essay, I suggest that what counts as *academic bravery* or *academic courage* is often contingent upon its uptake (i.e., whether it is recognized or not) and can be entangled in webs of privilege, and colonized by bureaucracy, even if the bureaucracy is labeled "democratic" or "feminist." If you are interested in the visceral, emotional, and intellectual unlearnings of inscribed oppressions collectively and, as Audre Lorde (1978) puts it, are unwilling to accept powerlessness, fly along. In fact, I invite you onto the supporting wings of communal bravery.

We achieve communal bravery through embracing resonance as a way of building an inclusive and multi-directional relationship. In my usage of the term *resonance*, I combine and modify the following two definitions of the term: (1) a quality of richness and (2) a quality of evoking response [due to its meaningfulness] (Merriam-Webster, 2017). This use of the term resonance allows room for the fragmented experiences to come together at different angles, since the lived experiences that inform our academic entanglements meet the moments of our new encounters of bravery in unexpected, often non-linear ways. Through resonance, the writer and reader create meaning together.

This project comes in pulsating and recurring dream vignettes, academic and non-academic. It comes in other visceral beats. It rocks back and forth (in time and space), as well as side to side (in time and space). The increasing and decreasing intensities that I am creating through these vignettes switching between the poetic-reflective and essayistic-reflective moods willfully abandon the linearity of time to tell a story that does not develop from Point A to Point B, but rather occurs as a result of different configurations of social locations.

Resistance in Flight

I wrote this piece in bursts over a period of a few months. Then, these executive orders came gushing from the office of the 45th ("Executive Orders," n.d.):

- January 20, 2017: Executive order minimizing the economic burden of the Patient Protection and Affordable Care Act
- January 24, 2017: Expediting environmental reviews and approvals for high-priority infrastructure projects
- January 25, 2017: Enhancing public safety in the interior of the United States
- January 25, 2017: Border security and immigration enforcement improvements
- January 27, 2017: Protecting the nation from foreign terrorist entry into the United States

In response to the executive orders above, two colleagues of mine organized a *Resistance Poetry* event for their students. I joined them with my students. We came to read-share writing that moved us as a way of dealing with a new reality in which those of us off of the Euro-Anglo American center, gender non-conforming, undocumented, non-white, and native need more resonance to withstand the slipping away of a movement towards a livable life. I came to read-share writing and song as a way of inviting folks to tune into an affective range of intensities on the wings of which we could all take off in flight to places where our imaginings of a livable life are a potentiality. So I first read this part that I had written for the *Counternarratives* anthology:

As a kid I had this visceral, paralyzing fear that someone was going to pull my fingernails and pour hot oil over them. Someone (the Turks, that is) is going to nail horseshoes on my soles, or that I could not save my kids by carrying them in the Syrian Desert as we walked and walked and walked. Being a latchkey kid walking and choosing my own books in a library to which neither the librarian nor parents paid much attention, I read volume after volume on the lived horrors of the Armenian Genocide. I listened to stories of long hair hanging on trees and gently rocking in the breeze after their wearers had jumped into bodies of water to avoid being forced.

I read all of this until it got in my own body, cutting away the decades separating the bodies experiencing these atrocities and mine. Now, decades after *that* Genocide and others, decades after my fear of hot oil poured over my raw skin and having read *Sophie's Choice* and *Zabelle*, and *1984*, I am thinking: *it is 9 degrees Fahrenheit and I am just wearing one layer of clothing in the house that is my shelter. How would I be walking on land in Syria, in Turkey, or Greece? How would I be rocking on a boat to Greece? I couldn't. I couldn't carry my kids on my back. What would I do? What would I do?*

I fall asleep in delirium. Again, it is this recurring dream that I have. In it, I am in a glass house overlooking the ocean. There is a biiiiig—no, huge— no, enormous wave coming. I am watching it get closer. I am having a hard time breathing. I am reminding myself that the house is safe, but I can not understand how I can think that when it is made out of glass the wave hits the house but does not smash it. Instead. It is pulling the house into the ocean. I can feel that I am sweating but I can not move or make any noise it is harder to breathe I see a wave wash a mass of people away I can not clearly see them I am not wearing my glasses but I can not get rid of this sense of urgency and panic. *This is the wicked witch of the global north*, I think. And, as I think this, I hear myself: *do I need to calibrate the scale of my rage in relation to the suffering I witness?*

After I finished reading, I kept rocking for a few seconds. Then, I sang a song in Armenian about longing and reaching for a hope that you can see as a potentiality. But every time you reach out, it either is not there or has morphed into a new situation in which you need to recalibrate yourself. I shared my writing and singing because the bravery of my students' creative wings supported me.

I had given my students space to explore what was meaningful for them, supporting them as they creatively traversed reimagined places in their own multi-genre autoethnographic works, which they did as part of their indi-vidual tutorials. And they had consistently blown my mind away by the powerfully vulnerable and brave engagements with traumatic histories of race, sexuality, and gender in their work that they publicly shared with oth-ers in reading, installation, and performance. Not only had they trusted my words supporting their boldness, but the power of their creativity had also had a profoundly transformative impact on me.

The creative courage of my students had encouraged me to take academic risks. Inspired by my students' creative courage, I had used singing as part of my research presentation at a major academic conference as an affec-tive methodology of sharing and generating visceral knowledge-experience. I took this risk as a way of experimenting with the advice that I had given to my students that seemed to have powerful effects in their own work, when I encouraged them to find openings for reimagining a potentiality. In the case of my conference presentation, I was looking for a potentiality, for a desired future in the present, as per Muñoz (2009), beyond political apathy in Armenia. This affective engagement with scholarship created a meaningful opening for me to further experiment with different genres of writing and thinking with my colleagues in Armenia. Later, I received a note from an art historian who had loved our experiment with multi-modal and multi-genre work and wanted to connect with me.

I am interspersing this text that weaves instances of communal bravery with lessons and strategies for moving others with one's own practice. These strategies are tentative, ever-shifting, contextually resonant, recurring, in need of doing things over, in need of refinement. They do not appear in a linear numbering order, rather as asterisks, because this could be the first strategy tried once, or many times over, but it could also be the 365th strategy tried. And, as Ahmed (2017) points out, strategy is not always and only a thought in action, but rather a thought refined through action. So, here is one I have been practicing recently:

Inspiration Strategy #*

I harness my creative courage, which I caught from my students, when I share my visceral knowledge through the sound of my (singing) voice. It has effects. It gets into bodies and creates attunements. I should pay attention to these attunements. They, too, have effects.

Bravery, then, much like gender and other performances, needs repetition to gain, sustain, and refine its own life-nerve-muscle. And, in this context of the *Resistance Poetry* event, this sharing of a visceral knowledge and experience was unexpected, running the risk of being picked up only as an emotional experience and confused vulnerability. Yet, to those present, my raw sharing within this particular political moment moved towards a refusal to repress confusion and succumb to isolation, and gave an option to fly, to imagine together. In other words, it was experienced, taken up, and recognized as a moving instance of public vulnerability.

Following the visceral images of my dream-sharing, the wings of my song created a world of intensities that allowed room for public vulnerability, and confusion, and frustration to be released as a way of building communal strength. I felt a quiet relief after I finished, a relief from my own helplessness. My colleagues and students indicated how touching and powerful the experience was. Everyone present seemed to have more oxygen to breathe. Or, should I say, they seemed to give themselves more permission to breathe? But this is not always the case. In the instance below, you will see how communal bravery emerges from a different kind of shared visceral experience.

Academic Non-dream

My college invited a guest to visit one of my classes—a Euro-American woman who identified as a women's rights advocate in Muslim-majority countries. "You need to open your mouth when you speak in public," she said to a student within a minute of her arrival. I heard my heart pounce. I—the Armenia-raised woman with the knowledge of feminisms of color—sensed the heaviness of her being a guest in my class, at my college, being an elder. I sensed and heard all these viscerally, but I did not hear myself saying: "I am not comfortable with the way you are speaking to my students."

"I was the [American] protector of our African students," she said within ten minutes of her arrival in the space my students and I had created to practice compassionate communication. After my students explained how we were trying to understand state violence, nationalisms, and social movements in post-Soviet space, she asked, "What about Islam that was suppressed during Soviet years and turned into violence after the collapse?"

I started up again. Ahmed (2017) tells me when we are able to start up again, we have a class and racial privilege. "I am hesitant to connect the erroneous media linkages of Islam and violence," I said. "I don't want to reproduce this damaging approach," I continued. I could start up again. I kept pulling my students into the text and the documentary on Armenian environmental activists resisting a mining company to build a mine in a village on the backs and lives of local farmers with faulty promises of short-lived unsustainable jobs. Our guest did not come to class prepared to contribute to the generation of knowledge for which we had gathered, even though I had sent her the material in advance.

Isn't this how colonization works? By taking over rather than contributing to the emergence of knowledge delinked from it? I could start up again. She had not read or viewed the material, so she did not have anything to contribute. I did not offer her space to say more things like, "I was surprised that people in Bishkek [capital of Kyrgyzstan, a central Asian post-Soviet country] looked Asiatic." I had taken away her privilege to say more things like, "One of my African students had a flat Mongolian face, as one of the parents was from Far East Russia. It was unusual to be Black and have Asiatic features." She felt oppressed. And everyone (Euro-Anglo and North American) heard about it. "She got under my skin," she said . . . to my Euro-Anglo, North American colleagues . . . to my Euro-Anglo North American administrators. This *she* was me.

Strategy #*

I need to get under a colonizer's skin more often.

But I did not hear myself saying, "I was not comfortable with the way you spoke to my students" until the next day in another meeting in which I heard how she "wanted to give you courage." This *you* was me. It was not until two days later that I would engage with my students in a self-compassion exercise as a form of communal healing, as a form of self-forgiving. Feeling a ra(n)ge of emotional intensities in my body, I shared with my students how unlearning the lessons of patriarchy is achieved with more ease intellectually than In. Your. Body. This is significant because, in reflecting on this experience, I realized how, in coming from Armenia, I had internalized not only the culturally conservative (communal) practices of honoring your guests and your elders, but also what counts as (individual) bravery: an immediate intervention. And, because I had not done that, I had immediately shamed myself. I had not recognized the other ways in which I had modeled an alternative way of populating the space with the anti-racist voices of my students rather than the racist voice of our visitor.

"How can we support each other communally in instances like this, when we are taken aback and paralyzed by our bodily inscriptions of various oppressions?" I asked. "It's a process," someone said. "I have learned to be gentle with myself," they continued. "Someone else's saying one word helps me," another offered. We were generating methodology from our communally shared experiences that had viscerally reminded us where we were with various inscriptions.

Emergent Strategy #*

We need to re-conceptualize bravery as a communally sustained practice.

By conceptualizing bravery as individual, I had foreclosed on *communal* bravery in action. Opening this space for cultivating communal practices nourishes individual strength, as well as communal attunement. We do this together. This is the *resonance* to which I was referring at the beginning of this essay.

What I am pointing to here is the emotional labor that it takes to viscerally act on one's intellectual unlearnings of how white supremacist capitalist patriarchy operates in one's many (non)academic lives, making us do its work of atomizing and disciplining ourselves for it. This labor of public vulnerability, self-exposure, sharing-as-teaching itself, while often unnoticed, *is* bravery and has effects. It builds communal resonance and attunements, and care. This care, as my fellow Armenian feminists Anna Shahnazaryan and lucine talalyan suggested in a yet unpublished interview-conversation, sustains the community as an alternative for a capitalist model of competitive individualism, which you will see enacted in yet another instance of communal bravery.

A Recurring Academic Dream

I am in a glass house overlooking the ocean. There is a biiiiig wave coming. I am watching it get closer. I am having hard time breathing. I am reminding myself that the house is safe, but I can not understand how I can think that when it is made out of glass. The wave hits the house but does not smash it. Instead. It is pulling the house into the ocean. I can feel that I am sweating, but I can not move or make any noise. It is harder to breathe. I see a wave wash a mass of people away. I can not clearly see them. I am not wearing my glasses. But I can not get rid of this sense of urgency and panic. *This is the wicked witch of the global north*, I think. And, as I think this, I hear: "We are sorry that you feel there has been some unfair appropriation of your work."

It has the same paralyzing effect that all my nightmares have: I sweat, I am unable to make a sound, I am unable to move, I can not breathe. Then, I burst back into the present. Back to the academic non-dream where feminist colleagues can take my words without asking and use them as their own in a feminist journal to discuss how the knowledge produced by scholars from "the global south" is not taken up as valid knowledge.

I follow-up, of course, by contacting the journal editors involved, providing evidence and dates. The editors go on to dismiss my charges, while simultaneously recognizing that there were instances of very similar wording.

I need to give you an important feminist context: my words appropriated without my permission were taken from a draft of an article discussing my research on the Queering Yerevan Collective (QYC)'s decolonial political artistic work. The QYC is a collective of artists, writers, cultural critics, and activists who use Yerevan, the capital city of Armenia, as an experimental space for their queering artistic activism (Queering Yerevan, n.d.). Besides appropriating my words, the decolonial feminist-identified scholars had also mis-named the QYC.

In this instance, I tried to challenge a senior feminist scholar—themselves self-identifying as *other*, from elsewhere and residing in Western academies—for their appropriation of my words. Yet, my effort was dismissed by democratic, ethical, and feminist self-identified academics. And here, Ahmed (2017) asks me to think about the kinds of knowledges I am generating by being in the academy that was not built (for me) with me in mind. I come to understand that dates and evidence, even if verified by many colleagues, are not enough to shift a colonizing (feminist) position. And the lesson I learn is this: we need to find ways to dismantle the discursive worlds that claim to be feminist yet accommodate colonizers. And I also remember the importance of my lesson about communal bravery.

To process this colonizing appropriation on our terms, the QYC, dear colleagues-long-turned-friends, and I engaged in an interview-conversation we titled "Թագա(հայ)տռում in flight: Singing tricksters, imposters, masqueraders." Unlike in our previous work together, where as a researcher I would initiate conversations and interviews, the QYC was asking questions of me in this project. We unsettled the feminist academic (mis)handling of coloniality of power disguised as conceptualization of decoloniality, by intentionally blurring the lines of the researcher/researched through our co-authorship, through multi-language and cross-disciplinary critique and self-reflection. This project was our way of embracing communal bravery. And as a result, we re-emerged with stronger communal attunements.

Strategy #*

Finding a space to speak our mind compassionately where we are attuned to our intellectual, visceral, and emotional experiences, abandoning the burden of respectability, creates an opening for an unwillingness to accept resignation (Lorde, 1978). We refuse to accept exclusion under the guise of civility (Ahmed, 2017).

I have been inspired by and have come to find resonance in my students, some of whom have been minoritized in some way and some of whom have come to realize the damaging effects of being majoritized. I have also been inspired by the deep care and practice of solidarity of my friend-colleagues. The readiness of my colleagues and students to hold a shared space for each other to be publicly emotionally vulnerable in the case of the *Resistance Poetry* event, developing communal care strategies after a visitor's disruption in the second case, and practicing critical communal care through co-authorship in the case of colonizing intellectual work are some of the ingredients of the bravery I traverse here, academic or not: a communally nourished affair, amplified by attunements.

Inviting and sustaining communal vulnerability and trusting the magical potential of communal flight, especially when the abstract intellectual accounts are insufficient without the visceral knowledge, creates a magical space of potentialities for taking risks to reimagine boldly and to fly. Together.

References

Ahmed, S. (2017). *Living a feminist life*. Durham, NC: Duke University Press.
Executive Orders. (2017, January). Retrieved March 23, 2017, from www.whitehouse.gov/briefing-room/presidential-actions/executive-orders?term_node_tid_depth=51&page=1
Lorde, A. (1978). Uses of the erotic: The erotic as power. In *Sister outsider* (pp. 53–59). Freedom, CA: The Crossing Press.
Merriam-Webster. (2017). In Merriam-Webster.com. Retrieved March 20, 2017, from www.merriam-webster.com/dictionary/resonance
Muñoz, J. E. (2009). *Cruising utopia: The then and there of queer futurity*. New York, NY: New York University Press.
Queering Yerevan collective. In *Queering Yerevan*. Retrieved April 12, 2017, from http://queeringyerevan.blogspot.com

Part III
Embodied Resistance
Counternarratives to Hegemonic Identities in the Academy

15 A Letter for Auntie Lorde

aja lenae johnson

yesterday I believe you
came to me in the form of a
woman at a podium telling me
tough skin is an ivory fallacy
in this tower stay, Tender
stay soft enough to long it is
the stuff of protest

when I was 17,
you told me I was
and that was enough and I believe you
but I am tired, I am a loud and angry tired
always wanting more,
draining from the weight of false
inquiry and individualism
faster than my age would tell

I wonder how far our promises of
new imaginings can carry me when I am so very soft
and I hold this unquantifiable longing still
this place aches a hostile womb for my old magic

my accomplishments caress the question
of cost and I remember the balm, your voice
telling me to hold tight to Dahomey
where we exist in a plane beyond
the gatekeepers' myths of knowing,
that this softness gifts my passage

16 On Being Powerfully Vulnerable and Why I Love My Black Woman's Tears

Kelsey Marie Jones

It won't be good. They won't like it and you are not made for this. Just look at everything that's come before you: smart, academic, creative, professional, worthy of publication. You are not any of these things and so you cannot produce the way you need to. You are not supposed to be here. And it's incredibly inconvenient because everything—*your whole life*—depends on what happens when your pen hits the paper, when your finger taps the key, when you decide the first word they will read. You imagine how they will laugh, grimace . . . there will be a rolling of eyes and gnashing of teeth. It will all come crumbling down around you and you will be forced to explain how you got here, how you snuck in, how you fooled them, how you made it this long and this far with so little to offer. Wild beasts will be unleashed; you will be hunted and cast out.

By the way, in case you are skeptical, this is all absolutely true and it will be that catastrophic (this is what you tell yourself at the first sign of optimism.)

But there is the slightest chance that this is an exaggeration, a distortion fueled by all of the times when your tiniest and most vulnerable self felt the weight of difference. Felt isolated, ugly, invisible, not good enough. Realized that this was how much of the world chose to understand you, as less than. And you were resilient in all of the ways we teach Black girls to fight back and resist: you developed strategies, you put on your armor each morning, you survived. Not good enough was not true.

And yet, not good enough persists. Not good enough . . . well, except for some things. Which things, again? Look! Even now it is hard for you to acknowledge your accomplishments, even now when you know not good enough is a myth. Deeply embedded, you are afraid of what it has already done. How much irreparable damage has it caused? Will it grow until there is nothing left in you for you to love?

Now, you understand—your armor is not effective. It did the work of shields and swords: it protected your body from sticks and stones, stopped you from falling apart. But it cannot protect you from what is happening inside; insecurity and not good enough reach and spread like a ficus, attempting to strangle and suffocate. They have been trying to steal you from you since you were a child. You have all of your pieces, but now it is time to bind yourself together, to be of stuff that is tougher than toughness.

I don't need armor to be strong. I am stronger than metal—three strands of my hair can break a bobby pin. I need to feel and touch who I am and the armor is getting in the way. It is too heavy, too cumbersome. There is humanity under the helmet, the breastplate and I need to care for it. I need air, I need to breathe.

To be brave is to shed the stoicism, fight the ficus, show myself, be bare. She said "Okay, now that you know, just do it." Well, of course. Obviously! Just do it.

> Like now, like what I'm doing now.
> Just do it, just write it,
> just write it down, write it down,
> writing it down.

* * * * * * * * * * * * * *

I can't remember the first time I cried in public, but I can tell you I've done it *many times* since then. I cry *a lot*. Like, all of the time. I would guess that I cry somewhere between two to three times a day, on average. I *love* to cry.

I am a Black woman just starting out in academia and I did not always love my Black Woman Tears. There was a time when my tears made me feel uncomfortable and ashamed. I was just too sensitive. My eyes watered at the first sign of discomfort, anger, sadness, embarrassment, happiness . . . any feeling you could name! It was the worst. My friends got in the habit of explaining my tears, saying "Oh, you know, that's just how Kelsey is." It was humiliating; I felt weak and out of control. I felt eyes on me and I felt ashamed; this wasn't just a professional problem, this was a *personal* problem. Clearly, there was something wrong with me.

We have been told that crying in public—especially in academia—is No-No Number One. Crying suggests that you are hypersensitive, hysterical, dysfunctional. In a word, *unprofessional*. The reactions to my tears confirmed that I was not strong enough, not good enough.

But I started to notice something about professionalism, about the rules of crying in academia. Some people could cry and still be heard! Some people could cry and be comforted! Some people had the power to stop a conversation for a minute, an hour, an entire semester, with a single salty drop! White Women's Tears could be personal, professional, and appropriate in a way mine could not. So I learned to apologize for my Black Woman's Tears and tend to the tears of White women. It is one of the easiest habits to fall into as a woman of color: generously and passionately caring for White women while saving shame and insecurity for yourself. But this is not about withholding compassion, this is about seeing yourself, about *being seen*.

* * * * * * * * * * * * * *

You See Me! Part I

I am sitting in his office, remembering to remember his name and his research and don't forget to make eye contact with great intention and zeal. In an interview, I want you to see how great I am. I want you to see that I am happy and agreeable and confident and perfect for your program. I see children's drawings on the wall and ask him about his sons—he has two and they are the same age as my students. He asks me how it feels to know that I am leaving my classroom so soon, what it is like to leave my students to be a student again. I search for the answers I prepared the night before, something about effecting change at a broader level and teaching teachers how to . . . do something. It doesn't matter, it's already happening. I am crying and I am not stopping and all I can get out is that "it is hard," and it is clear that I am not ready to fully process this question.

Shit!

My armor is cracking and I am shocked by how quickly my emotions have betrayed me. The shame starts to rise up in my throat but my tears know better; my humanity is breaking through, demanding to be seen. *I want to be seen.* He nods his head and sits forward in his chair. There is a pause. Instead of a tissue, he hands me two books on positive development for youth that I never give back. He asks me about my students, what they are like. He understands. He sees me. In fact, he sees me so clearly that he invites me to join his program and I decide to make it my home.

You See Me! Part II

I am rushing to another office, trying to forget the words that were said to me on the street. I feel violated and unprotected and *so angry*. But I need to focus on sounding smart, proving that I belong here, that I will be the best doctoral student he has ever seen, that I am not an imposter. I rush in and he asks me how I am doing. I want to talk about the research, but it doesn't matter. It's already happening. I am crying and I am not stopping and the hurt that grows with every catcall and invasion of my space flies out of my mouth. I cannot believe this is how I am starting the first meeting with my advisor.

Shit!

I feel embarrassed and uncomfortable with this level of emotional exposure. I try to find "professionalism" but my tears are gentle and firm—my humanity wants me to heal. I cannot heal if I am busy hiding. *I need to be seen.* He shakes his head and leans back in his chair, makes some "hmm" noises. He asks me how I am feeling and I realize he is giving me permission to be angry, to process the sadness that comes with being put on display without your consent. He understands. He sees me. We talk about what I need and how I can respond in the moment, what my comeback lines will be. I use them and then he teaches me how to teach them to other Black women. All of a sudden—and not-so-suddenly—I am emotional *and* strong.

You See Me! Part III

I am in class and we are sharing data. These data are about a young Black couple and we are thinking about ways to understand their experiences and their relationship as a family. I am listening and then there is a shift; the class has decided that these young people are abusive and abused, pathological and doomed, incapable and "interesting." I am ready to speak up and interrupt the conversation, my heart is pounding and I hear the words strong and clear in my head. It is my turn and I open my mouth, but my eyes open, too. I am speaking and think that maybe if I open my mouth wider and turn up the volume, I can distract my eyes and they will dry up and leave me alone. But it doesn't matter, it's already happening, I am crying. I am not stopping.

Shit!

I have been taught to conceal my anger and so I am surprised by its quick and easy arrival. I have done so much work to suppress my anger because the fear of becoming an Angry Black Woman is overwhelming. These lies are powerful but my tears are fierce; my humanity wants me to advocate for this family and for myself. *I choose to be seen.* She invites me to her office after class and we talk. She makes time for me to hear my concerns and echoes them with her own. She understands. She sees me. She addresses the class the next week and does not open it up for discussion; I realize that this is about protection. She is a professor setting boundaries and protecting *me* so that I do not bear the weight of these interactions alone. I will not carry this anymore.

* * * * * * * * * * * * * *

When I cry, I am demanding that you recognize my humanity and *see me*. Sometimes, there are people who cannot see me because they don't know how or seeing me makes them uncomfortable. That is hard, it is painful. And yet, there are other times when I am seen so clearly; this is when I find the people who wrap around me, comfort me, remind me that I am part of a community that wants me to be brave.

To embrace emotion is to embrace the power of vulnerability. It is a risk to make myself vulnerable in academic spaces, knowing I may be seen as angry, militant, out of control. But I cannot be successful in my work without acknowledging the incredible influence of that vulnerability on my research and teaching practices. I cannot separate my emotions and personal self from my professional self because my work is deeply and beautifully emotional. *I am deeply and beautifully emotional.* My emotions are not only at the center of why I do my work, but also build the foundation of how I do my work. I will not and cannot be silenced or shamed by my feelings; showing emotion is an act of resistance. It is about celebrating my humanity, even when the academy would rather I stay dehumanized. It is about remembering who I was before I got here and how amazing it is that I *still am.* What a beautiful thought, that in all of my power and vulnerability and strength and emotion, *I still am.*

* * * * * * * * * * * * * * * *

There is pain in realization.
A sharp ache when you understand that the rules are only meant
For you.
That they can rip you apart
Question your very being
And tell you to observe and absorb with
No comment.
And fix your face, too, they might think you are
Angry about something.
They prepare each other for your presence, they have to practice how
    to feel when they
See your skin.
Hear your voice.
Read your words.

You are the trigger!
They pull at you, pull at you until you explode! and
    then they ask you
"Why?"

To live like this, it is
Not good enough.

You are not dangerous
Well, not in the way they think.
You have weapons of your own
You keep them in the places they told you to empty
To hide the bull's eye so the pain had no place to land.
But you knew better.
You remembered to remember.
You stored them away and
They are still there, memories vivid and faint, stacked high
Easy to open, tricky to unpack, but look, count them.
Sturdy and loyal,
They are all there.
They are waiting for the day you are ready to be brave.

Do you remember?

Do you remember that you are
Strong.

Creative.
Powerful.
Determined.
Brave like a Black woman who knows how to cry.

Crying for sadness, for joy, for anger
Crying because I feel like it and because
I can.
I am a beautiful crier.
I can cry! I can cry! I can cry!
Like those kids and the fairy who lost her voice to a man who
    forgot to grow up.
Thanks, Tinkerbell, but you can keep your dust
I run on Black Girl Magic.

17 Vulnerability

The New Brave

Natanya Ann Pulley

It wasn't until the third or fourth day of my first teaching colloquium as a grad student that the class finally talked about appearance. Along with the university's policies, requirements for teaching a core writing class, and tips for success, I just wanted someone to tell me how to dress for a profession into which I did not feel that my body would fit. I wanted to hear from my female peers and colloquium advisors; and I wanted to hear that women professors (and especially women of color) don't need a tailored and armored persona. But they didn't say such things. And I immediately shut down a fearful part of myself—a part vulnerable and anxious of all of the ways in which I was asked to not be human, but a performer. I invited a new robot version, a pod version that would nod about the problems with cleavage, with dressing too smartly or too grubbily, about colors and heels and why skirts. Women, especially women of color, can't let up when it comes to image, they warned. Like I'd be walking into a pack of hyenas while covered in Lady Gaga's meatgown.

After the discussion on dressing for success and upon realizing that I was too short, fat, brown (but not brown enough), and maybe a little too laid-back punk-goth-and-nerdy to be respected by my students, one of my peers in the colloquium whispered to me, "just wear whatever you want," which suggested that I can be daring, and daring felt brave. At the time, I nodded and thought: *sure, you can say that because you are white and a man and pretty good-looking and already have a trendy, but grounded sense of style.* I still do think this from time to time—the way in which my male colleagues can wear jeans, blazer, and a button-shirt and call it good. Ironed or not. Worn or untucked. For the third or fourth day in a row or not. And I've tried to replicate a female version to no avail—my breasts and delusions about my body get in the way.

However, I am not writing this essay to focus on fashion. As a creative writer, I'm in the fringe area of academia. I can get away with a little more by claiming to be artsy and prone to emotional outbursts manifesting in some heavy black eyeliner and oh-so-many black blazers and cardigans. But I bring up this memory to remind myself of what it was like to be told how important appearance is for woman of color in academia. To remember those early days of imagining that there was a way to best present myself that is informed, fair, and true—a way that could be instilled in me by speaking with mentors, advanced grad student peers, and by visiting countless websites on the subject. I really believed that there was one good way to appear professional in academia until I neared graduation and fell into the job market madness. One worried and insomnia-ridden night, I realized how quickly a discussion on dangly versus non-dangly earrings at a Modern Language Association (MLA) interview could wormhole into 100+ comments and replies on a job market advice blog. It wasn't just my sense of calm that was at stake during this time, but the advice I received from academia was that I needed to conform to an image to succeed. I needed to not just pretend to be more confident than I was, but to abolish all manifestations of personality, quirks, and especially insecurity. To a graduate student, being brave in academia meant shedding my nature, hardening myself, and ignoring my own vulnerability.

This approach comes from two specific messages from colleagues, articles, and institutional ethos that I continually hear. I've been blasted and burdened with the message that I should be myself, as well as the message that I need to be careful of who I am in a classroom because I am a woman of color. The first notion makes sense for an extrovert or non-first-generation academics or someone who fits easily into the sort of boxes created for professors. I've always wanted to be the cool professor (casual, but still nice jeans, cool T-shirt, signature blazer) who sits on the desk to talk to his students. But I can't find the just-right jeans, shirt, blazer combo for my shape; and I'm short and overweight and am afraid of hopping up on a desk only to slide off and break myself. The first message can be confusing because it sounds like it should promote confidence and composure, which is only true for those who are easily confident and composed. Over the years, I've amended the message to mean: be myself as much as one can be in the academic world of skill, smarts, talent, and performance. And it's okay if this "self" takes some years to find or changes along the way because it will take time to become comfortable with one's own vulnerabilities especially in a setting that suggests they are a weakness or defect.

The second message is a labyrinth of both fact and fallacy. *Be extra careful as a woman of color* sounds realistic and wise because it does come from numerous examples of women of color being disrespected, abused, assaulted, and humiliated in the classroom by students and colleagues (and history and text) alike. It is true that a woman of color faces different challenges than individuals from other groups. It is true that women of color work harder than others to be acknowledged as equals. It is true that what can be read as quirky, casual, badass in a white male professor might be read as weird, sloppy, and bitchy in a woman of color. And yet this advice puts the burden on us alone to change the climate of academia, which can be debilitating. If one is continually assessing their conduct, appearance, and personality under this warning, the urge to discount vulnerability and to see bravery as only something blunt like a weapon or armor is astounding.

After my first-year of teaching as a tenure-track Assistant Professor, I realized that the worries I had about appearing confident and brave were not just thoughts or feelings. Rather, they had become active in my body as nerves, stress, and migraines. They took up space and time and calm (and my health). Juggling all of the advice that I'd received and policing myself had become as much work as all of the meetings, answering emails, teaching, and grading. It wasn't the life I wanted, and it was also unsustainable. I would worry myself ill, frustrated, angry, and uninspired. I needed to make a change, but I knew I couldn't simply turn off the worry or feelings. Instead, I stopped feeding them, but would acknowledged them as I would clouds in the sky—part of the weather system of myself, which could whir itself up into heavy winds and threatening nimbostratus if I let it. When I felt drawn to over-criticizing my performance, attire, or how I carried myself, I would acknowledge my own vulnerability and say aloud, "this job is hard sometimes," and I'd let that truth sit in the room with me a few seconds. Then, I'd find something on my list of things to do that felt rewarding or utilized my best strengths.

For the most part, this strategy has worked through some overworked years at one institution and in the uprooting and bumpy shift into another. I found a version of myself that wasn't the robot or pod person whom I created in grad school, but a healthy balance of self, persona, inspiration, and utility. It's mostly sustainable and it is its own type of bravery. The type of bravery that isn't the glint of a sword or standing when my spine is screaming me down. It is an everyday type of bravery, the kind of bravery that is like a well from which to drink each morning. It isn't about standing up for what one believes in the face of danger or putting one's body in the line of fire to save another. It's about knowing that each day will have its challenges—some of which seem to be specifically directed towards my body, gender, race, or age. And, yet, still I enter that space to be there for my students and to become a part of a larger discussion in which I deeply believe. It's about knowing that I could get away with the bare minimum or I could shy away from teaching the more challenging and volatile texts or I could slink through meetings and events giving only the smallest parts of myself, and instead choosing to put myself out there, often feeling exposed or vulnerable.

My days of assuming vulnerability is a weakness or defect are over. The world fears vulnerability because being vulnerable means acknowledging our own limits and risking our strength and securities. Vulnerability becomes a mislabeled twin of ignorance—if one is vulnerable, then the world can feel comfortable calling them unaware. It makes it easier to imagine vulnerability as a lack rather than a mode of being. Yet, vulnerability is not the same as being emotional or without healthy personal boundaries, though we tend to think of it that way. If we wrap vulnerability up as a flaw, then we don't have to deal with its truth and how it exposes our desires and needs when facing opposition.

When I think of things vulnerable, I imagine raw buds near blooming. Of that ghost quiver of a string when first pulled. A soft untouched skin soon to be made solid by the hand of another. Yes, I think of areas of a wall that show signs of crumbling. But I also see a moment of possibility—a moment that dares to have no wall or to point out the futility of such a wall. I think of those seconds when I have a feeling amorphous and immense, before I label, symptomatize, and seek to change, accept, or filter it. The pupa exoskeleton weakening and the expanse of butterfly wings not yet a reality.

Many professors and instructors fear showing this vulnerability, which, if read as a weakness or as unprofessional, can result in not only direct challenges or dismissal from students, but dissension or even threats. The curated poise and authoritative persona, then, is accepted as appropriate armor in academia, and I use it from time to time, as well. But also, I've made room for my vulnerability and the vulnerability of others, which means being brave enough to show my emotions. This does not necessarily mean that I bring my entire range of emotion or my whole sense of self into the classroom, office, or a meeting. But I do listen to the ways in which my emotions tug at me and I am open to the emotional landscape—this multifaceted terrain of insecurities and desires—surrounding me. I don't cater to emotions or allow them to pummel my objectives or others, but I do feel they have a long-term place in academia with me.

While embracing vulnerability in academia is a lifelong endeavor, some moments speak louder than others for me. And I'm always surprised when, despite my daily engagements with this certain kind of bravery, I am thrown off by my own emotional response. Recently, a nervous student was sitting in my office. A sociology major, I think her desire to write seemed selfish to her and she was unconvinced that it was worth her time to develop—or perhaps was scared to admit that her work was worth her energy and mine. She rarely made eye contact until she asked whether she could ask me something possibly inappropriate. I said that she could ask, but I might not give a direct answer. She inquired whether I ever discouraged a student from writing and more pointedly from taking writing courses or "becoming a writer" (that magical moment of fairy godmother and Cinderella-like transformation, I guess).

I began to tear up. While my instinct was to hold my emotions back, I didn't. I wasn't overcome because of any personal challenge I felt from her, though I did feel cast suddenly as all-out authority as well as gatekeeper, ally, cheerleader, spiritual guide, aggressor, saboteur, and enemy to my students. Rather, it was a very sad question that broke me open because I cared so much for writing and for anyone's dreams to express themselves in writing and the idea that I (or anyone) could stand in the way of that was heartbreaking. I knew that in this moment I could show this sadness or I could hide it and leap to an answer common in the literary community about advising writers. But I didn't just want my student to know that I deeply cared about my students and writing. I also wanted her to know that sad questions with heartfelt answers have a place in my office as well as in my life. I wanted her to see that vulnerability leads to answers.

I told her that it's heartbreaking to think anyone has the power to dissuade another from something as personal as writing—speaking, hearing, and making the self live again on paper. My voice broke apart at times. Sudden moisture, then air, then dryness throughout my throat. The tears slid about and around my eyeballs until I knew they'd start to fall out of me, down my face, which would also mean my nose would start to run. It was not a pretty cry. All hot skin and soggy with deep breaths to pull the heartache back in. To take away someone's voice simply because I had the credentials and experience and absurd ambition and a lot of luck seemed too cruel a reality. The student could tell that I was shaken and that I was speaking from a vulnerable place—trembling and raw—a difficult place to defend because the emotions ran so deep and strong to undo the stability I work to build with students.

In the days following this instance, I had a hard time remembering that bravery and not weakness allowed this moment of vulnerability. I've had to be brave among my peers, students, and colleagues in ways I believe are more obvious: calling out discrimination, bias, and hostility, standing up for others and myself, or introducing fraught texts or ideas. Bravery allows me to reply to a student or colleague's belittling or offense when I'd prefer to run. And bravery helps me to raise my hand and provide an opinion or suggestion when I'm fairly certain that it won't be entertained. But the kind of brave I'm most interested in these days is the vulnerable kind because it isn't about critical thinking, facts, or compromise. While speaking up amongst colleagues and administration has been difficult for me, I can usually turn towards the data, the proven analysis, or the objective of the group or community. What I risk in those situations is an opinion or approach, but not my sense of self. Instead, I'm interested in the type of bravery that is willing to shake loose emotional foundations, to see what fossils and mineral veins are the strongest and which can grow stronger despite the threat against them.

To be clear, I'm not advocating for relieving one's emotions and inner self in a classroom instead of informed critical discussion. I'm not advocating for showing a softness in order to appeal to anyone or in an effort to prove one's humanness. Nor am I suggesting we throw out healthy boundaries or measured responses. But what I'd like to think is that somewhere in those weeks of training for a new profession, someone would have said: being brave doesn't mean ignoring or discounting parts of one's self. It's not about posturing or presenting a persona shaped by fear. Being brave means standing up and speaking when you'd rather run away, yes, but also it means embracing one's vulnerability in order to find a way that fits you best and honors what you hold valuable and vital even if our culture would call that way weak or lacking. This willingness to embrace vulnerability will look different for each individual. It may be in revealing more emotions or allowing them to inform one's choices more. It may be in recognizing the vulnerabilities in others and finding ways to be comfortable around them. Perhaps it will appear in accepting one's own instincts and reactions as valid expressions worth accepting. Or, for the grad student I was, in letting go of the idea that clothes can shield me enough from being as sensitive as I am. I now strive to be brave enough to not only face my vulnerabilities, but to allow them to be assets in my teaching and my life.

I think that one of the most basic tenets of education is acknowledging the areas in our research, curiosity, and imagination that need developing. We push ourselves and our students to step on shaky and unpredictable ground in order to sort out what can be secured with facts, scientific method, and careful and informed analysis. We seek to dispel ignorance—this lack threatening our future. And we tend to turn this approach towards human emotions; we can choose to see them as a lack of productive material rather than recognizing and celebrating that when we feel weak or exposed, we may be closer to a truth and sense of self than ever before. To provide room for that which makes us and others feel exposed (be it feelings of insecurity, anxiety, hurt, or disappointment) is a strength and an act of bravery that isn't always about one instance, but many and throughout the day.

As the student in my office that day saw my tears and detected a slight tremor in my voice, she said, "sorry, I didn't mean to upset you." And, while looking upset means showing I am vulnerable, I took a deep breath and explained that I wasn't upset by her or her question, or at least not upset in the way she might think. But I was simply reminded of how tricky it can be not only working in the arts and as a professor, but working with the hopes and growth of others and myself in general. And it's good to be reminded of that from time to time. I'd be more concerned about myself if I forgot or ignored or avoided how vulnerable we are all—about how much we long for acceptance and acknowledgment and the ways in which we are always operating within our insecurities. What's the point of being smart, skilled, educated, talented, and capable if we aren't also soft, malleable, and always at risk? Being exposed and embracing vulnerability helps me see what drives me and what I fight for every day. It's a good thing.

And she, a bright and thoughtful student afraid of committing her voice to paper, agreed.

18 Undocumented in the Ivory Tower

Alessandra Bazo Vienrich

As an undocumented immigrant in North Carolina during a time when Latinx immigration was new to the state, it did not take long for me to realize that my racialized ethnicity, combined with my immigration status, influenced how people perceived and treated me. This knowledge informed my understanding of the obstacles that I encountered as I navigated the college application process in a state that did not offer tuition equity for undocumented students. Yet, it wasn't until I became aware of the intersections among my gender, racialized ethnicity, and immigration status that I began to understand how these identities shaped my journey in higher education.

In recent years, I have become more vocal about my immigration status in academic spaces. Now a PhD candidate in sociology, I am keenly aware of how my identity as an undocumented Latina has influenced how I experience life in the ivory tower. My experiences with discrimination have shaped every step of my academic journey. Yet these experiences have also helped me to find inspiration in the struggle inherent in being an undocumented student, instructor, and researcher. In seeing the struggle itself as a constant source of bravery, my journey in academia has been validated by my experiences of survival and thrival despite being excluded from some academic spaces and opportunities.

In this essay, I discuss my experiences in academia as an undocumented Latina student, researcher, and instructor. I reflect on times when I relied on bravery to continue moving forward in higher education, and highlight the different ways in which liminally documented[1] academics like myself can negotiate their immigrant identities and find the support necessary to harness their own bravery. My hope is that this essay will resonate with graduate students and early career academics who are undocumented, unDACAmented (i.e., those who have benefitted from Deferred Action from Childhood Arrivals[2]), and those who have other liminal immigration statuses, such as Temporary Protected Status (TPS). The strategies I provide include taking ownership of immigrant narratives in academic spaces, the role of "coming out" as a source of bravery, and finding meaning in the academic journey itself.

From Fear to Bravery

Since I first arrived in the United States, my immigration status has been something I was taught to hide, to be ashamed of, and to treat with caution. After all, this single fact about myself had the potential to harm me, criminalize me, and result in my deportation. It was because of my immigration status that I was unable to obtain a state driver's license and was required to pay out-of-state tuition at public colleges and universities. My undocumentedness was so present in my life that it seemed necessary to remain in the shadows just to maintain a sense of normality for my family and me in the midst of the anxiety associated with our precarious immigration status. In a context with increasingly restrictive immigration policies and practices, and where the threat of deportation was eminent, I hid my undocumented immigration status in order to survive. Being "in the closet" about my undocumented status was crucial to minimize the possibility that I would be forcibly removed from the country, barred from returning to the US, and separated from my family indefinitely.

Though DACA had been announced by the time I began graduate school, I was not able to benefit from this Executive Order until many months later. As such, my decision to continue my journey in academia preceded DACA and was filled with the uncertainties associated with being an undocumented student unable to receive federal or state financial aid, or to even apply for student loans. The fact that being undocumented made me subject to a 10-year bar[3] upon leaving the US also prevented me from applying for a work visa after graduation; I would first have to go to my country of origin to request it. This meant that, even if I could find a way to afford graduate school, there were no guarantees that I could successfully practice my profession in the US after completing my degree.

As I prepared to pursue an advanced degree in sociology, it became clear that even if I were accepted into a graduate program, there were a number of factors that would hinder my chances of enrollment as an undocumented student. I knew that my ineligibility to legally work would prevent me from pursuing teaching or research assistantships, and I wondered whether that might affect my ability to thrive in my graduate program. The expenses associated with a graduate education exacerbated this concern. From meals to books to transportation, my financial responsibilities extended well beyond graduate tuition and fees. I had experienced financial instability before, but I had never done so without a support system around me. I worried that losing my support system would further intensify my financial precariousness as an undocumented student. Knowing that I might be hundreds of miles away from my family, in a place where the cost of living far surpassed the small financial contribution they could afford, made going to graduate school seem unattainable. And, like so many undocumented students before me, I asked myself, "Is it really possible for me to go to graduate school while undocumented?"

Despite these risks, I remained undeterred in applying to and ultimately attending graduate school. Pursuing a graduate degree was more than getting an education for me. Taking this path meant that I did not have to leave the place I called home to pursue my dreams. Surely, I could have left the US and searched for educational opportunities in my native Perú or in other countries, but pursuing education in the US was assurance that I could stay home on my own terms. It meant that, within the endless constraints associated with my immigration status, I could have agency in determining my future. I found the courage to commit to pursuing a graduate education, in knowing that taking this path meant no longer letting my immigration status rob me of opportunities that were seldom afforded to students like me. The fact that I was not even supposed to be in these academic spaces, that people like me did not go to college, much less graduate school, did not limit my drive to continue going forward and to become one of the first undocumented students to earn a PhD.[4] I knew that being included into academic spaces challenged the status quo by bringing people like me into spaces where our existence as college-educated individuals was often unknown, and where the possibility that we could pursue advanced degrees was seldom considered.

My desire to embark on this journey from secrecy to scholarship was also partly driven by my longtime commitment to social justice, particularly justice for fellow undocumented immigrants. Living in North Carolina exposed me to the economic, political, educational, and social exclusion experienced by undocumented immigrants and fueled my desire to eradicate these exclusionary practices. And the anti-immigration and xenophobic climate at the national level further influenced my decision to pursue graduate school, as I witnessed undocumented student-activists march in Washington, DC, and build momentum for their cause in the years following the introduction of the DREAM Act[5] to Congress. I was determined to become a scholar who could publish research on the conditions of the undocumented immigrant population in the US South, providing data that would inform national immigration policy.

As a way to minimize the risks associated with my decision to pursue graduate school, I strategically reached out to one of the few Latinx staff members at my college. I felt that, as a Latina, her views on undocumented students might be more progressive and this motivated me to trust her with the fact that I was undocumented. She acted as an ally in my plans to pursue an advanced degree in sociology and took it upon herself to explore my financial options, reaching out to graduate admissions, program directors, and faculty members at prospective universities. Her help aided me in navigating the graduate application process and finding institutional funds to pursue a master's degree in sociology. Having this staff member as an ally and first point of contact was paramount in minimizing the risks of pursuing graduate school, and reassured me that, with the right help, it was possible to go to graduate school while undocumented.

"Coming Out" as Undocumented in Academia

As I left North Carolina to begin my graduate studies, I also left behind many of the risks that prevented me from being open about my undocumented status. Much of my fear about "coming out" as undocumented was rooted in the xenophobic and anti-immigrant sentiment present in North Carolina at the time and the impact that disclosing this could have on my family. Although some of this fear still lingers with me today, leaving that context and my family behind gave me a chance to confront the potential personal and professional consequences of disclosing my immigration status. The competitive, sink or swim culture of academia had made me afraid of the possibility of being further doubted, further questioned, and having to work even harder to prove myself in academic spaces. After all, when it came to my education, there was no Plan B and "coming out" had the potential to put into question my legitimacy and my place in the academy.

Yet I realized that the alternative to coming out was not being true to my identity. I had reached a point in my life when I was ready to incorporate my undocumentedness into the whole of my identity, to no longer hide this important part of who I am. I was fully aware that, at best, disclosing my undocumented immigration status might lead to impertinent questions and uncomfortable interactions with professors and fellow grad students in my department. At worst, it could jeopardize my ability to receive institutional funds to cover the cost of graduate tuition. But, for the first time in my life, I was giving myself permission to shape my own narrative, deciding that coming out would no longer intimidate and scare me.

My time as an instructor for a course on immigration, teaching a group of adult students at the only public university in the city of Boston, gave me a platform and the motivation to begin the process of coming out as undocumented. Having the opportunity to teach at an institution with a large immigrant student population allowed me to witness my students' bravery in the classroom as they shared their own immigration stories. They talked about their experiences with race relations in Boston as immigrants from Haiti, revisited the hardships their parents and grandparents faced as immigrants from Ireland, and one student even shared his feelings about his own identity as a Mexican-American whose Mexican ancestors became Americans after the US annexed part of Northern Mexico following the Mexican-American War. These stories inspired me to share my own immigration story in the classroom. It was time to go a step further and embrace my full identity in academic spaces where my racialized ethnicity, sexual orientation, gender, accent, and nationality were all things that I already embraced and shared openly. In the end, bravery came down to the most fundamental aspect of my being: my identity.

The validation that I received from my students after disclosing my undocumented status gave me the courage to continue sharing my immigration story with faculty and fellow graduate students. The feeling of relief and the weight that came off of my shoulders when I began to reveal my undocumented status in academic spaces was something that made me wonder whether I could have experienced this sense of freedom sooner had I disclosed this information before. Taking ownership of how I disclosed my immigration status allowed me to feel that I was in control of my own immigration narrative and prepared me mentally and emotionally to publicly disclose my immigration status. After all, coming out meant doing something that could not be undone. To share with my peers and colleagues a fact about myself which might very well be used against me.

I found that disclosing my immigration status required a specific set of conditions that helped me manage such an emotionally overwhelming process. Whether it is an advisor's commitment to being an ally and advocate in the department, or the solidarity of fellow graduate students by demanding that undocumented students be accorded the same funding and opportunities for research and teaching, the decision to come out should be accompanied by a support system that serves as both a source of emotional support and practical advice. I sought the support of fellow undocumented students, many of whom were undergraduates, as well as the support of faculty of color. It was these individuals who helped me deal with the feelings of guilt over whether I should have disclosed my immigration status sooner that emerged after I finally made public my undocumentedness.

While it takes bravery to negotiate the sharing of such an important and central aspect of one's identity, this is something that should be done only when mentally and emotionally ready. My journey to "coming out" as undocumented was one that required years of self-reflection and the emotional support of family and friends. Perhaps the most important part of coming out was my own realization that I had to do this for myself. No matter what the reactions of academics were, coming out was a path to a life free of secrecy and fear, and one where the sense of liberation that I feel today would extend to both my personal and professional life.

Reflections on Undocumented Women Academics: The Path Forward

My path to becoming an academic has, by no means, been one of unwavering courage and resilience. There have been times when fear has taken over my ability and willingness to continue pursuing a PhD in sociology, to publicly embrace my undocumented identity, or to be my own advocate in academic spaces. What has remained constant is my ability to find value in this unique journey and to maintain my desire to embrace my full identity as an undocumented Latina in my different facets as a grad student, researcher, and instructor. My roles as researcher and instructor have continuously served as sources of inspiration as I continue to navigate unknown spaces in the academy. As I move forward as an ABD ("all but dissertation") doctoral candidate and take on more responsibilities as an instructor, I am confident that my experiences with bravery in my different roles will help me better serve students, especially those who are undocumented and liminally documented.

As I think about the future of my research on undocumented immigrants, I also see the value in my ability to be my own advocate. As a graduate student nearing the end of my doctoral program, I am no longer challenged about my academic choices, as I was a few years ago. I have found that in discussions with advisors, professors, and even as I seek funding for my dissertation research, I act as an advocate for my research as I seek to preserve its integrity and essence without jeopardizing its true purpose of giving undocumented immigrant students a voice. Nevertheless, I am aware that there will come a time when I will once again be at the start of something new and I will be ready to advocate for myself.

In writing this essay, I have come to the conclusion that thriving in the academy, as an undocumented woman of color, is more about surviving every step of this unmapped journey than about achieving traditional academic milestones. Recognizing the value in all accomplishments, no matter how small, and having the ability to look at one's progress through our own eyes, is what makes thriving in academia a reality for the undocumented. It is in seeing our perseverance and courage to navigate the academy that undocumented women of color redefine the meaning of thrival.

Notes

1 "Liminal legality is an 'in-between' status in which immigrants possess social security numbers and work permits but have no guarantee of eventual citizenship" (Cebulko, 2014, p. 143).
2 On June 15, 2012, the Obama administration released a memorandum allowing undocumented immigrants who came to the United States before the age of 16 consideration for deferred action. Under Deferred Action for Childhood Arrivals (DACA), undocumented immigrants who meet certain criteria can apply for temporary relief from deportation. In addition, DACA beneficiaries are eligible to apply for a social security card and a temporary work permit; documentation that is likely to facilitate their access to institutions of higher education (U.S Citizenship and Immigration Services).
3 The ten-year bar prohibits reentry of immigrants who accumulate "unlawful presence" in the United States, leave the country, and want to re-enter lawfully (American Immigration Council, 2016).
4 In May 2016, Yuriana Aguilar became the first DACA recipient to earn a PhD (Tate, 2016), and in March 2017 Gloria Montiel defended her dissertation at Claremont Graduate University (Peña, 2017). As of June, 2017 they were the only DACA recipients to have earned a PhD.
5 First introduced in 2001, the Development, Relief, and Education for Alien Minors (DREAM) Act, was proposed legislation that would have made a large population of the undocumented youth population eligible for a path to citizenship.

References

American Immigration Council. (2016). *The three- and ten-year bars* [Fact sheet]. Retrieved from www.americanimmigrationcouncil.org/research/three-and-ten-year-bars

Cebulko, K. (2014). Documented, undocumented, and liminally legal: Legal status during the transition to adulthood for 1.5-generation Brazilian immigrants. *The Sociological Quarterly, 55*(1),143–167.

Peña, M. (2017, April 4). After breaking through barriers, DACA recipient sets sights on giving back: She was the first student from Santa Ana High School to attend and graduate from Harvard University. *NBC Los Angeles*. Retrieved from www.nbclosangeles.com/news/local/After-Breaking-Through-Barriers-DACA-Recipient-Sets-Sights-on-Giving-Back.html

Tate, A. (2016, June 8). Student is first undocumented immigrant to get Ph.D. from UC Merced. *NBCNews*. Retrieved from www.nbcnews.com/feature/college-game-plan/student-first-undocumented-immigrant-get-ph-d-uc-merced-n587406.

19 A Latinx *Testimonio* of Motherhood in Academia

Patricia Herrera

When I was young, my mother would take me to the garment factory where she sewed clothes destined for department stores. I had the unfortunate job of unthreading the garments that were sewn incorrectly. In that dark, noisy garment factory, women workers shared stories about how they arrived in the United States, the hardships they faced as Latinx immigrants, the many preconceived stereotypes that their boss had of them, and the aspirations they had for themselves and their children. It was there that I first heard my mother tell the story of how she came to New York City for her honeymoon, visiting on a student visa granted through an Ecuadorian governmental lottery. Tears skated down my mother's cheeks as she shared how she had left behind her friends, family, and community to start a new life. My parents grew up poor, but they had worked hard to change their destiny by pursuing a college education in Ecuador. My mother was studying to be a pharmacist and my father an accountant. Now that they were living in the US, going to college did not seem like an option. My parents left with the dream of working as much as they could in America, saving up and eventually going back to Ecuador, but they never did. After thirty years, they are still on their honeymoon.

My parents' stories make me aware of the profound ways in which culture has shaped my personal and professional life. I use the style of *testimonio* to document, share, and theorize my lived experiences of struggle, survival, and resistance, a practice firmly rooted in a Latina feminist methodology (Latina Feminist Group, 2001). As Maria Castañeda and Kirsten Isgro argue in their 2013 anthology, *Mothers in Academia*, *testimonio* deepens the ways in which we understand the impact of gender, race, sexuality, and social class, and how the practice can serve to intervene in the social, political, and cultural life of academia. The process of reflecting on the complexities of my professional and personal identities is a means of participating in the production of collective knowledge and consciousness (Anzaldúa, 1987; Godínez, 2006).

With this in mind, I share my story. A *testimonio* about my experiences as a working-class first-generation Latinx immigrant mother in academia. A *testimonio* about successfully completing my PhD, obtaining a tenure-track job, and parenting three children despite the silent shroud of judgment and stigma I faced from advisors and colleagues, as well as family members. Through this *testimonio*, I hope to empower mothers, especially Latinx mothers, to navigate academia with a strong sense of self, intentionality, and courage. I share the lessons that I learned from being a mother and an academic to underscore the gender biases, racism, and cultural barriers operating in academia and our everyday lives.

Honoring, Yet Resisting, My Cultural Traditions

Bravery looks and feels very different for each of us. How I handled motherhood as a graduate student pursuing a tenure-track faculty position did not always look brave by mainstream standards. It was not always aggressive, confrontational, or even outspoken—adjectives that we often assign to bravery—for those traits do not necessarily jive with my personality, cultural upbringing, or even who I am. In many ways, to become both a mother and an academic required me to honor my cultural traditions while simultaneously resisting the constraints they imposed upon me.

For example, when my family responded with concern when I announced that I was pregnant with my first child, I was faced with daunting task of respecting our cultural values while also pursuing the best path for my family and my career. Often my mother asked, "Couldn't you wait [to have children] until after you got married?" She then followed that question by bringing up the time she felt betrayed because she found out from my college boyfriend's mother that I had lost my virginity. From that day on, every time I would visit, my mother would lovingly caress Baby, the Chihuahua we had during my college days, while cooing to her, "you are the only virgin in this house. You are the only one who kept your legs closed and did the right thing, not like Patricia." This was the anthem my mother sang every time I saw her while I was in college. And she remorselessly sang it when I announced that I was pregnant with my first child. By that time, Baby had long passed, but my mom sanctified her as the family virgin—her way of prying open an old wound of betrayal.

Like many immigrants, my parents believed that, with a good education, many opportunities would open up, so they encouraged me to pursue a professional career. But they felt that I shouldn't be *too* professional, especially if that would mean that as a woman I would be neglecting my *familia*. In my Catholic upbringing rooted in Ecuadorian traditions, marriage, motherhood, and *familia* rank high on the list of expectations placed upon me. Because my mother could not conceive of the idea of my finishing graduate school while raising a child, she advised me to give it all up and take an easier route. "Why not get a job as an elementary or high school teacher, Patricia? Your work hours will be the same as your children's schedule. You will have summers off with your children and the benefits are good. Good salary. Good health insurance. It would be good."

While I could have simply given in to my mother's judgment and become a teacher or avoided my family's shaming by interacting with them less, my cultural values were intimately linked to my *familia*. Instead, I chose a more difficult, third path—to honor my cultural traditions while also resisting them. I continued to maintain close contact with my family because of my strong feelings of cultural loyalty and *respeto*, which meant facing judgment daily, but I resisted these cultural norms by pursuing motherhood and a PhD simultaneously. Staying connected with my parents was often uncomfortable and uneasy because I was never going to give in to their ideas of who I should be, but I was not going to stay away either.

Flaunting My Pregnant Body

By starting a family during my graduate studies, I knew that I also risked defying unspoken—and sometimes clearly spoken—norms about motherhood in academia. In particular, having children and pursuing an academic career were viewed as mutually exclusive choices. I resisted these expectations by continuing my studies while also deciding to follow my heart to start a family. And I didn't do so quietly—I decided to fully embrace my pregnant state by unapologetically flaunting it.

I was under no illusion about how my pregnancy would be viewed by fellow academics. Faculty in my program regularly advised women students against starting a family during graduate school because, they warned, babies would only slow them down and ultimately sideline their pursuit of a degree. As a result of this gendered narrative about motherhood, many of the women faculty either timed their pregnancies to avoid conflict with their academic responsibilities or put off having a child. Many also chose not to have children, regardless of the social and cultural expectations placed on women to become mothers. I was instructed to choose between academia and motherhood. And, if I chose to be a mother, I was failing to prioritize my professional career.

A few days after sharing the news of my pregnancy to my graduate school community, a white woman faculty member shared an article with all graduate students through the departmental listserv. Though it was common for faculty to share news about our field on the listserv, this particular article was about how women graduate students who get pregnant are less likely to finish their graduate training. When this went out to everyone, the wagging finger was no doubt deeply felt; it was a hard slap in my face and it stung. The message conveyed tremendous doubt that she and other people in my program had about my ability to make it through. The imprint of this slap never really went away; I consistently felt additional pressure to prove that I could finish my PhD, even as a Latinx soon-to-be-mother.

While I did not personally confront the professor who sent out the article, I decided to respond to her in the best way I knew. As a theater practitioner, I understood the power of the body. I decided to flaunt my round belly in a department that was patently anti-pregnancy, anti-baby, and anti-mother. Even as my body was the site of so much judgment and stigma, it became a site of empowerment and resistance. Since I had completed my comprehensive exams, I still had to get my proposal approved and that meant going to the department and meeting with my advisors. I made sure to wear my most fitting tops that accentuated my round, low belly on the days that I met with them.

On one of those days, I first stopped by my mother's house. As she opened the door, she looked at me in shock as if I my appearance was sacrilegious and welcomed me with a *"¡Virgen Santisima! ¿Que estas puesta?"* (Good Heavens! What are you wearing?), while making a sign of the cross. When my mom was pregnant with my brother and me, she wore giant shirts or dresses that concealed her belly; pregnancy was something to hide. But I chose to outright flaunt my belly for the world to see. My mom's negative response to my flaunted belly was exactly the response I wanted to evoke in my department. My body was loudly speaking—"I am pregnant and I will finish!"

Every time I came to the department, I had to confront all of the percolating doubt and shame coming from faculty and fellow grad students. When I visited with a male advisor, he never asked about my pregnancy or how I was doing. He always immediately provided feedback on my proposal. Since he seemed uncomfortable or oblivious, I felt impelled to connect my scholarly progress with the fact that my belly was growing, especially since it was more and more visible with the passage of time. I attempted to set a new precedent for the beginning of these meetings by sharing with him how far along I was with the pregnancy and how I was dealing with it before he proceeded with his feedback. But that did not work; he automatically went on feedback mode. So, I politely interrupted him and said, "Before we get started, let me tell you how it is going. I am six months pregnant now and it's harder to sit down to write for long periods of time, so I stand." I proceeded to tell him that it was impossible for me to detach my scholarly productivity from my *re*productivity. My belly reminded me that I had to finish my dissertation proposal. Despite how many times he forgot to check in with me, I repeated this ritual. Eventually, with my unabashed belly popping, my dissertation proposal was approved and the next phase of graduate school had run its course.

Though I challenged the stigma of motherhood in academia by flaunting my pregnancy, I was aware that the odds of finishing my PhD were even slimmer while juggling the demands of caring for a newborn. One way I sought to minimize the risk of stalling my progress was to find academic allies who would be able to support me in the process. The first person in the department to whom I disclosed my pregnancy was my main dissertation advisor; I met with her to share the news and to ask for her support, advice, and guidance on how to be a mom in graduate school. She had a daughter, so I hoped she could share some words of wisdom. The minute I uttered the words, "I am pregnant and am due in August," concern crept into her eyes. Yet she stood up, elated with joy and caringly hugged me, dousing me with congratulations.

But she was quick to give me a reality check. She asked, "How do you plan on finishing?" Then, concern crept deeper in her voice as she proceeded to sketch out a timeline of dissertating while pregnant. As we sat together in the sanctity of her office loaded with shelves full of books, I nervously asked her, "how did you do it?" Just the fact of having a woman's ear and advice was a tremendous aid that I could not have done without. Her voice warmed up as she confided that she was a single-mom when she started her tenure-track job. The only way that she made it as far in her career as she had was to put structure in her life. She revealed, "every Saturday, I went to the library and worked 9am-5pm, while my child was with her babysitter." She religiously worked in this manner to finish the article, the book, earn tenure, and get promoted. She charged me to come up with a timeline and a routine that would work for me. This advice set the stage for me to eventually defy others' expectations that I would leave grad school with a baby but no degree.

Publicly Nursing My Son

Just as I flaunted my belly to disrupt anti-pregnancy norms in academia, I continued my defiance by publicly nursing my newborn baby in similarly anti-mother and anti-baby academic spaces. I grew accustomed to regularly challenging what it meant to be a Latinx mother in graduate school—again, by refusing to separate motherhood from academia. Specifically, I challenged the hegemonic expectation of feeling discomfort in doing what comes naturally to me as a mother while in public spaces.

The decision to nurse publicly in academic settings began almost immediately after the birth of my first child. Just ten days after giving birth to my son, I had to attend a daylong orientation for a competitive writing fellow position for which I was selected after successfully defending my dissertation proposal. I could have simply skipped orientation to recuperate and care for my newborn son. However, I decided to go because I did not want to give my supervisors any reason to question my ability to fulfill my responsibilities. Nor did I want to give the impression that I was an academic lightweight who needed to take it easy because I just had a child.

Orientation day was a blur. I was sitting in a gigantic auditorium full of graduate students while my ten-day-old son started to whimper and root around my chest. I cuddled him, hoping that would soothe him, but that did not work. My heart started to beat faster when I realized that the moment I had been avoiding was now here. I had to nurse my son right then and there because that was the only thing that would calm him down. As discreetly as a new nursing mother could, I unhooked my nursing bra, rocked him into a cradle hold, and attempted to put my nipple in his mouth.

I prayed that he would instantly latch on and quiet down, but my nipple slipped a couple of times out of his mouth and his cry got loud enough for people to begin to stare. I had this terrifying image of all eyes on me—eyes not necessarily welcoming my ten-day-old tiny wonder of the universe, eyes not necessarily welcoming me. And, as I struggled to latch him on, I realized that he was having trouble because I felt uncomfortable about nursing in a hostile space. I was sitting near students who had once doubted my ability to get this far. I took a deep breath, got comfortable, and affirmed that the only authority on my body was myself. As I properly positioned my breast for my son to latch on, my relationship to academia as a Latinx mother and student forever changed.

Nursing in public meant that I experienced a lot of judgment and disdain when I went to my university's library, cafeteria, departmental or administrative offices, and other places on campus. However, despite this knowledge, or rather because of this, I persisted with this practice until it no longer felt strange for me to do so. I chose to resist with my body, working with and within my body to not only feed my baby, but also to challenge the academic hegemonic space and create pathways for myself and other new moms.

Demanding What I Need as A Nursing Mother

While I was completing my dissertation, my second child made me aware of the power of my nursing body. My daughter taught me how to unapologetically take risks—namely, asking for what my family and I needed, even if it could mean losing out on professional opportunities.

After the birth of my daughter, I had been a graduate student for over six years and the idea of finishing my dissertation with two children at this rate seemed nearly impossible. If I was going to finish, I needed to focus exclusively on my dissertation and the only way that was going to happen was if I applied for external dissertation fellowships. Fortunately, I was invited to do a phone interview for one of the fellowships for which I applied and subsequently was invited for an on-campus interview. I was ecstatic about this opportunity, but when I saw the itinerary I realized that I had not entirely thought through the logistics of dealing with my young baby, who was still dependent on mother's milk. I stared at the itinerary for my campus visit, hoping to find some way to sneak in a nursing getaway with my daughter, but it seemed impossible. The visit was packed with meetings with faculty and students, yet I had no plans of leaving her behind or weaning her that early.

My first child taught me to lead with my body and not be discreet about my pregnancy and nursing. But I was unsure how I would do so when I was on a campus interview. I wondered whether I would risk my candidacy if I were open about being a nursing mother and brought my baby on the interview. This was another moment when I could have easily left my child at home and not have said anything at all, but my nursing body ached every time I imagined being away from her. I had already decided not to put my child's well-being at risk for a dissertation fellowship. I decided to continue to refuse to prioritize my academic career over the needs of my family.

I riled up the courage to call the chair of the dissertation fellowship committee. My cold, sweaty hands dialed the number and my voice quivered as I first thanked the chair of the fellowship committee for coordinating all of the planned meetings. Then, I explained that I had a nursing baby and that I would be bringing my infant daughter to the campus interview. I assured her that I would be making arrangements for someone to come with us so that she could be taken care of while I was interviewing—but that I would need nursing breaks.

There was a pause in the conversation; as I nervously waited for a response, I heard my heart beat faster. By asking for this accommodation, I was challenging what it means to be a mother in academia. I knew that mentioning my daughter would bring judgment and could implicitly erode my academic credibility, but I wanted to create a family-friendly alternative for myself and possibly other academic moms. Interestingly, the chair shared that this was the first time that she had encountered a dissertation fellow candidate with a nursing baby and that she would need to get back to me with a plan. Within half an hour, the chair returned my call with a new itinerary that accommodated by needs. I was relieved but anxious about how it would go. I spent more time reviewing the schedule to make sure that I knew when I would need to quickly get to my room than on fully investigating faculty members' portfolios. In theory, the odds were against me because academic mothers are less likely to advance up the ladder. But, a week later, I received a phone call with the news that I had been accepted as a dissertation fellow.

Accepting the external dissertation fellowship was also a bold decision. It meant leaving New York City and the network of people who had supported me. While many theater practitioners would love the opportunity to be in New York with the many available performances, I was willingly leaving. For my partner, it meant resigning from his job. It also raised a whole series of questions about housing, childcare, and parenting. Since we did not have a support system at this new location, babysitting was going to be challenging and the cost of childcare was above our budgetary means. We made the unconventional decision for my partner to be the stay-at-home dad to ensure that I would finish my dissertation. As a one-income family, the only way that we made ends meet was by enrolling in the Women, Infants, and Children (WIC) program. Socially, it was lonely and challenging—for my partner because there were hardly any men who stayed at home, and for me because fellow mothers perceived me as neglectful since I was never around during the day. Deciding that my partner would be a stay-at-home dad was an economic sacrifice but, in the long run, this was the best way to proceed if I was going to close the chapter of my life as a graduate student. This choice got me through writing the dissertation, through the job market and, most recently, through earning tenure.

Walking Forward in Life Even When There are So Many Unknowns

I learned I was pregnant with my third child during the last year of my dissertation fellowship. The news came as a complete surprise. If one or two children can put having a successful academic career at risk, having three children might seem like self-sabotage. But the birth of my third child taught me how to courageously walk forward in life even when there are so many unknowns. At the time, I was anxiously applying to as many jobs and post-doctoral fellowships as possible. As in the case of my first two pregnancies, I was overjoyed, but also overwhelmed by questions about how I could finish my dissertation. I reminded myself that I could prioritize my family while completing my graduate studies when I was fortunate to receive several offers, including a post-doctoral fellowship at the institution where I was. I decided against uprooting my family, instead staying for one more year where I had also received my dissertation fellowship. I defended my dissertation in the summer and filed it in the fall, and started the post-doctoral fellowship. My third child was born that April.

Graduation was scheduled in May—six weeks after I gave birth. At first, I did not want to participate in graduation. I was utterly fatigued. Besides, what did I have to prove? But the truth was that I had worked so hard to get to this point, to earn a PhD while having three kids along the way. I had chugged along without taking any real maternity leave because I feared losing out on any opportunities. There was no way that I was going to allow anything to stop me from honoring myself and celebrating this moment.

My partner, three children, and I headed back to NYC so that I could walk across the stage and get my doctorate. Throughout the graduation ceremony, I remembered the many moments that came with judgment and shame when I decided to start a family, but after ten years and three babies, I was finally holding my PhD. There I was, walking with my cap and gown, carrying my latest bundle of joy snuggled in my Maya wrap. Picking up my diploma while carrying my one-month old infant was yet another public statement—"I am a Latinx mother who did not fail from graduate school." I could hear my partner, parents, and friends cheering for me from the audience when my name was called. That was one of the proudest moments in my life.

The professor who sent the email out about pregnant graduate students failing out of their doctorate program approached me with a gift in a departmental reception. The feeling of the stinging slap resurfaced, but this time we were face to face. Our exchange was brief. There was no apology from her end, but I knew her gift was her way of trying to alleviate that slap. I did not formally thank her, but told her that I would always remember this day.

I placed the little gift box on top of my altar as a reminder to me that no one can or should get in the way of my personal or professional dreams. The little box remained there unopened until I moved to my first job at the University of Richmond, where I am now a tenured associate professor.

Throughout my journey as a Latinx first-generation college and PhD graduate, I have dealt with the judgment and stigma that comes with being a Latinx mother in academia and tell this story of resistance, resilience, and bravery. The births of my three children have taught me important life lessons of how to mother bravely as a Latinx woman in academia. Each child came at a different phase of my graduate career, giving me the strength to move forward with more and more courage. My first child amplified the importance of culture even when I went against the grain. He taught me how to embody resistance by choosing to flaunt my pregnant body and nurse in academic spaces. My second child taught me to take risks for what I need unapologetically even if it meant ruining my chances of getting a fellowship. My third child taught me to courageously walk forward in life even when there were so many unknowns. And forward I go, every day a new part of this journey.

References

Anzaldúa, G. (1987). *Borderlands/la frontera: The new Mestiza*. San Francisco: Aunt Lute Books.

Castañeda, M., & Isgro, K. L. (2013). *Mothers in academia*. New York, NY: Columbia University Press.

Godínez, F. E. (2006). *Haciendo que hacer:* Braiding cultural knowledge into educational practices and policies. In D. Delgado-Bernal, C. A. Elenes, F. E. Godínez, & S. Villenas (Eds.), *Chicana/Latina education in everyday life: Feminista perspectives on pedagogy and epistemology* (pp. 25–38). Albany: State University of New York Press.

Latina Feminist Group. (2001). *Telling to live: Latina feminist* testimonios. Durham, NC: Duke University Press.

20 On Desiderata

Alta Mauro

Be careful. Strive to be happy.
The last line of Desiderata¹ reads:
Be careful. Strive to be happy.
But what if I am through with striving
and toiling
and straining
and the scraping and scrimping of life?
What if I insist on life—
abundant life—
without labor and pain
and downcast eyes?
We Black girls have grown weary of the stress
and the striving
the bondage
the pain
the obliteration of even a false hope
the promise of faith in the face of despair
the comedy of trust in a world in love with deceit
the error of believing when "show" never meets "prove."
We Black girls.
Our mothers gave themselves over to striving
and taught us the same
as much with their words-
written in sweat and in tears,
smeared across filthy windowpanes
that blocked out the light
or maybe that trapped it in. . .
Our mothers
y nuestras abuelas,
they showed us to our place at tables reserved for our kind
but we heard tell of a girl like us
who turned over the table when she was told to sit-
stormed out and left the dinner to grow cold.

She said she'd rather starve on her own terms
than to thank them for this lesser portion-
first growing full but then growing sick
their poison rolling around in her belly.
We heard about her,
saw her shadow behind our reflection,
felt her looking back at us when we stared up into the clouds,
sensed her wrap her strong arms around us when they came
 to strip us naked,
heard her whisper confirmation when consolations would not do:
Head up, Black girl,
and grab your quill.
Across your heart
hope not to die-
pen a new proclamation that says to self and sister
"Take back your yoke and bitter being. I choose myself and
 life—together."
And we-
we Black girls,
may we suggest you take a page from our dogged determination to
 life?
In a new version of your well-intentioned—if intentioned
 at all—prose
end, instead, with this:
"To be happy-
Thrive."

Note

1 Ehrmann, M. (1952). Desidertata.

Afterword

Archana A. Pathak

An anthology such as *Counternarratives from Women of Color Academics* is both groundbreaking and foundation-building. It not only disrupts a variety of hegemonic structures, but it also speaks into existence imaginings of a world in which we "respect, honor and celebrate differences" (Audre Lorde[1]). It does so by offering strategies, possibilities, and plans for structures framed in and through justice.

Reading this anthology has been a deep shadow journey into my memories and a renewed affirmation that, while all does not happen for a reason, I have been able to find purpose in all that I have experienced. I am a 1.5-generation South Asian Indian-American diasporic woman who is the daughter of immigrants. Born into an upper-class, upper-caste family, I was brought to the United States at the age of four by my parents. I identify as a Hindu, middle-class/bourgeois, queer, cisgender, femme without disabilities for whom the relentless pursuit of social justice has been the focal light that has guided my professional career. It has also deeply shaped my personal life, at times in painful ways.

My quest for justice centers around the multitude ways in which I have learned and known difference. The hope that "there must be someone else like me out there" is the fuel that drives my entire scholarly career. *Counternarratives* mirrors these feelings and offers a space that holds them. It offers affirmation, language, and theory for my experiences. The plurality of voices are each individually important and collectively offer pathways for our success. This text reminded me that I have succeeded by disruption, by persistence, and by redefining and renaming success. In honoring these gifts, I humbly offer my reflections on this anthology in no linear order. Each one a breath—complete in itself and a part of everything before and after.

Sharing Our Stories and Claiming Our Space

Many of us make sense of our experiences by studying them (bell hooks). Despite history keeping our stories out, struggles of women of color, people who are queer, gender non-conforming, working-class, first-generation, indigenous, non-US/non-Western, and disabled are documented at times and are gaining visibility in spaces beyond their own communities. However, this visibility is a double-edged sword. There is a way in which our stories are sometimes co-opted into a "trauma drama" that feeds the beast of liberal, well-meaning folks and organizations attempting to be "allies." What is meant to serve as "critical witnessing" (Tiffany Ana Lopez) becomes a siren call to prove the "wokeness" of privileged folk.

Like bell hooks, I wanted to study the South Asian diaspora because I *needed* to understand my world. Understanding my world was/is a layered process. Of course, I want to make it meaningful for those outside of it, but more poignantly, for myself and my community, I want to embrace its complexity and richness. I want to center its fullness in ways that go beyond the dominant, oppressive read of it. To interrogate my world is to practice disruption, reclamation, and resilience. This anthology serves as a home space for my critical, de/colonial, feminist methodological self. It whispers to me that I can, and must, keep writing in my voice, and that the outlets for my voice exist and are open to receiving my work. As we all heed this call, I envision the emergence of bodies of literature that are as vast and diverse as our identities and experiences.

However, when we document our stories, I want for us the ability to protect those stories. And, at the same time, I do not want to put our stories of suffering on a pedestal. We are not merely our struggles. This anthology develops a discourse that both addresses the way our stories are co-opted while also offering a reclamation of our stories. Our stories are as complex, complicated, diverse, and contradictory as we are. The diverse contributors capture that vibrancy of difference and complexity, demonstrating that our many ways of being can be shared ways.

Visioning and Building a De/colonial Academy

A work like *Counternarratives* brings immense value to the academy as an epistemic structure, to marginalized peoples within academia, and to those who see themselves reflected in the academy. It first disrupts and then re-imagines the academy in terms of its intellectual agenda, institutional structure, and pedagogical commitments. It continues the ongoing project of de/colonizing the academy, similar to the writings of Kakali Bhattacharya. This anthology offers succor to marginalized communities by naming our experiences and providing and modeling strategies of resilience and success.

The women of color who contributed to this anthology utilize multiple genres and diverse voices, crossing disciplinary boundaries and framing intellectual/scholarly work outside the arcane "ivory tower" modes of production. As Aph and Syl Ko reflect in their kitchen table conversation, the violence of the academy begins at the epistemic, methodological, and disciplinary levels. By putting into publication through traditional academic modes of production such stories, epistemologies, and methodologies, this anthology provides a powerful resource on which to continue building an academy owned by all of us, where our work is not "alternative."

The chapters herein reflect the thoroughness and disciplinary rigor that is the nucleus of interdisciplinarity, from Robin Zape-tah-hol-ah Starr Mint-horn's pushing back against mainstream academic norms to Nancy López's building of an interdisciplinary institute. As done in this afterword, I invite us to examine our politics of citation and disrupt "rules" that minimize and/ or silo our voices. As we do so, we begin to rewrite the rules that bind us. Performance artist Nora Chipaumire taught me that we build and demand discipline in our work so that we can then be free. Building our intellectual disciplines rooted in our traditions frees us to be full members of a transformative academy.

Resilience, Strategies, and Contradictions

Counternarratives highlights the full journey of hurt, contemplation, rage, persistence, insistence, and building anew that many women of color academics experience. It allows for our humanity while celebrating our heroism. From Robbin Chapman's poem, to *La Colectiva*'s mentoring program, to Roxanne Harlow's "answering the call," we see the ways that we continue to *be* even when we are invited to disappear. We see how seemingly contradictory truths shape our lives. In the face of attack, we engage with vulnerability (Natanya Ann Pulley). In the face of loss, we speak our truth (Alessandra Bazo Vienrich). When mocked, we embrace our authenticity (Kelsey Jones).

By publishing work focusing on key strategies, successful programs and modeling ways of being that are often read as impossible (Yolanda Flores Niemann, Robbin Chapman, and Patricia Herrera) these women counter the spurious critique that marginalized communities overdetermine oppression and underdetermine agency and transformation. Reading these pieces transported me to pivotal moments in my journey when mentors stepped up and stepped in to nurture me, challenge me and model for me the power of claiming my truth, even if it seemed that doing so would cost me everything.

I recall attending a conference panel discussion on issues of feminism in Communication Studies as a young, overconfident graduate student. Brashly, I called out the senior scholars on the panel (a veritable "who's who" in the field) for not teaching and mentoring young feminists like myself. But, after the panel ended, Dr. Brenda J. Allen, one of the field's leaders, sat with me and listened to my story. She acted in ways contrary to what the academy would deem necessary or deserved; though senior, she approached me directly, thanked me for my comments, and asked me to meet with her. She was not affiliated with my program; she was not connected to any of the faculty with whom I worked. But she decided to engage my critique. She acted with her power in ways that nurtured me, guided me, and showed me with compassionate clarity what I needed to learn. She was patient as I worked my way through my own understanding of relationships between senior and junior scholars. She invited me to trust myself, especially in terms of what it meant to be a woman of color in the academy. Her interventions were incisive questions phrased so clearly and gently, especially when they focused on helping me understand my missteps. Though we lived in completely different parts of the country, she responded to my calls and emails; she always makes time for me at conferences. Months can go by, but responses to my communication are always warm and welcoming.

As Dr. Allen models, we women of color consistently and persistently shepherd each other because we know and understand that these choices go beyond helping individuals; they serve to build infrastructures of inclusion and justice. Despite everything in the system, in our training, and in our professional relationships that tell us not make certain choices, we do. Because we *know* it is right, it is just, it is necessary. For us, social justice is a moral and ethical imperative (Gilda Barbino). Resisting oppression is not a choice we make; it is a life we live. This work shapes our healing (aja lenae johnson, Tayler J. Mathews) and reflects our commitment to transformation. We honor our ancestors while building for our children, training those who come after us, advocating for those who walk with us, utilizing the power we have to build broader bases of shared power that heal the toxicity that can permeate the academy (Janelle M. Silva, Nelli Sargsyan, and Kandace Creel Falcón).

Going Forward

As a non-tenure track, term faculty member who holds a part-time administrative position in my institution's diversity and inclusion office, I will utilize this anthology to continue building diversity and inclusion policies and practices that center voices that have too long been left in the margins. As a postcolonial feminist scholar and teacher, I will utilize this anthology to teach ideas that resonate with many of my students, but rarely achieve scholarly legitimacy. Through this text, we will talk about our voices *as* theory rather than our voices as *opposed to* theory. As a partner, friend, family member, community member, and activist, I will share this anthology with others in moments when I feel they, too, can benefit from *Counternarratives*. I see this anthology as both an answer and an invitation. It answers the need for traditionally recognized modes of scholarly work while simultaneously inviting us to build beyond the limits of the academy.

Counternarratives of Women of Color Academics is distinct because of its multiple uses throughout the academy. The diversity and depth of voice throughout the anthology makes it an ideal text for a variety of spaces in the academy, ranging from traditional classrooms to student development, as well as faculty training and mentoring. This anthology can serve as a guidebook for young women of color just learning to navigate the academy and as a tool for the people guiding those young women. Simultaneously, it is a scholarly text that theorizes the experiences of women of color, providing foundational work on which the academy can continue building a canon of scholarly work in which voices of color are framed and read as scholarly, central, meaningful, and critical to the intellectual agenda of all scholars. Additionally, it offers those in the dominant structure vocabularies and narratives to know us in our fullness, rather than through a monochromatic narrative of suffering and/or resistance.

Counternarratives is both a model of, and theorizes about, the ways our personal, activist, and scholarly lives exist simultaneously and intersect. As women of color, this anthology invites us to live beyond mere survival. It calls for us to frame our lives through our complexities, nuances, strengths, and resiliencies. It offers us a blueprint to read ourselves as centrally and intrinsically belonging in academia and intentionally moving in the world that way, rather than merely continuously attempting to prove to others that we belong. We are called to create work that energizes and affirms us, that claims and names our space in the academy. What would it feel like if every journal, every book, and every discipline valued the voice and perspectives of the essays and poems found in this anthology? We must dream big. We need to continue bringing into fruition (print and otherwise) our stories of resilience, thrival, success, failure, and living through it all. It is time to live unfractured lives, where our academic, activist, and personal selves are our whole selves.

Counternarratives from Women of Color Academics implores us to realize that we are meant to "Be happy—thrive" (Alta Mauro).

Note

1 I name several key scholars in this afterword. My intention here is to invoke the entirety of their work rather than a single piece. To that end, I do not include a reference page and invite readers to be with these scholars in their fullness. We build on a rich history, indeed, a canon of work. I invoke the foundational scholars who shape my work by name rather than by specific works. When we are introduced to white male scholars, we are taught them by name, invoking their entire body of work. That is true here for our great thinkers, as well.

Contributors

Gilda Barabino, Dean of the Grove School of Engineering, the City College of New York

Gilda Barabino is a transformative leader and distinguished pioneer who is internationally recognized for her biomedical engineering research on sickle cell disease and cartilage regeneration, contributions to the modernization of university-level STEM educational practices, and her innovative approaches to diversifying the academy. She has accomplished a number of remarkable firsts in her career and is currently serving as Dean of the Grove School of Engineering at the City College of New York, and in that role is the first African-American woman to serve as dean of engineering at a majority institution.

Robbin Chapman, Associate Dean for Diversity, Inclusion and Belonging, Harvard Kennedy School.

Robbin Chapman grew up on a farm in Dinwiddie, Virginia, and moved to Brooklyn, New York, when she was nine. Whether on a farm or in the city, she indulges her love for science, reading, and exploration, and especially for lifelong learning. This has led to lots of adventures, like teaching piano to senior citizens, working with a NASA Space Shuttle group, and volunteering at after-school technology centers.

Bertina H. Combes, Associate Dean for Academic Affairs & Research and Professor of Educational Psychology, University of North Texas

Bertina H. Combes is an African-American mother, daughter, sister, and friend whose daily life intertwines these aspects of her being with her work as an academic. As the daughter of university professors, she learned the transformational power of education in the lives of her parents, family, and community members. Sharing the power of education by mentoring and helping others navigate the academy is a value that she learned from her parents and endeavors to pass on to her own children. Her interest in studying individuals with differing abilities is also generational, shared by her parents and her children.

Alicia Re Cruz, Professor of Anthropology, University of North Texas

Alicia Re Cruz is a scholar, professor, mentor, mother of three wonderful
Latino boys, and wife, and she is proud to intersect these roles "with
her own accent." Much of her professional life has been colored by her
efforts to create and be part of "communities"; this has been the survival
strategy that she learned in *El Puente de Vallecas*, a low-income barrio
where she was raised in Madrid. Anthropology is her life's work, the passion to learn from people, to work with people, to create a philosophy
of "togetherness" which for her is the effective tool for social justice and
equity. Her experience with the immigrant, refugee, and asylum seeker
communities of north Texas are a constant creative inspiration for her
work philosophy and ethics.

Gerry Ebalaroza-Tunnell, PhD Student in Transformative Studies and Consciousness, California Institute of Integral Studies

Gerry Ebalaroza-Tunnell is the daughter of Roy Ebalaroza and Gloria
Felimer. Born and raised on the island of Oʻahu, Hawaii, she is the third
child out of six. She now resides in Bothell, Washington, with her husband Jeremy Tunnell and their five-year old Belgium Malinois. She is the
mother of two grown sons, Edward and Ryan, and the grandmother to
a wonderful eight-year old little boy. Gerry is currently working towards
her PhD in Transformative Studies and Consciousness at the California
Institute of Integral Studies.

Kandace Creel Falcón, Associate Professor and Director of Women's &
Gender Studies, Minnesota State University Moorhead

Kandace Creel Falcón is an avid food photographer and curator of fine
tequilas. She lives in rural Minnesota with her *Vaimo* (Finnish-American
wife) Liz and growing brood of animal companions on twenty acres.

Eric Anthony Grollman, Assistant Professor of Sociology, University of
Richmond

Eric Anthony Grollman (they/them/theirs) comes from a family with a legacy of Black women organizing for racial and gender justice. An activist
turned academic, Eric has committed to using their scholarship, teaching,
and mentorship, and service as vehicles for social justice. Fresh out of the
traumatic experience that was graduate school, they launched a blog for
marginalized scholars—ConditionallyAccepted.com—which was later
picked up as a weekly career advice column on *Inside Higher Ed*, eventually becoming a national platform for those on the margins of academia.
They launched Sociologists for Trans Justice, which aims to advance the
project of transgender liberation in and through sociology. Eric lives in
Richmond, VA, with their partner, Eric Knauff.

Roxanna Harlow, Founder and Executive Director of Higher Learning, Inc. and Assistant Professor of Social Sciences, Carroll Community College

Roxanna Harlow is a Black woman sociologist, teacher, activist, advocate, and social entrepreneur at Carroll Community College in Maryland. Her interests are in race and ethnicity, education, social inequality, and social justice. She's a walking contradiction—a shy and introverted rule-follower placed on this earth to do work requiring public speaking, educating, agitating, standing up for others, and challenging the status quo.

Patricia Herrera, Associate Professor of Theatre, University of Richmond

Patricia Herrera is. . .

The daughter of garment workers who emigrated from Ecuador

The mother of three amazing children

A theater practitioner and educator using theater to engage with issues of social justice

An incredible force full of strength, passion, and drive.

aja lanae johnson, BA in Ethnic Studies, Ronald E. McNair Scholar, California State University-Sacramento

aja lenae johnson asks, "What can it look like to 'get free,' affirm our magic from the margins, and fuck with the greys?" She is a working-class, Queer, Black, multiracial woman, an artist, an activist, and a first-generation academic. In all of her endeavors, she explores belonging and the creative genius involved in building bridges across our fears . . . how those of us who were never meant to survive craft spaces to thrive.

Kelsey Marie Jones, Postdoctoral Fellow, Racial Empowerment Collaborative in Applied Psychology and Human Development, University of Pennsylvania

Kelsey Marie Jones is a Black woman born to two wonderful Black Jamaicans (Maureen and Tony), along with a beautiful little sister named Kaila (she's an amazing Black girl). Kelsey has had the privilege of teaching fantastic students. She loves her work and is learning what it means to bring more of herself to her research and her practice. Oh, and she loves to cry.

Aph Ko, Associate producer of the documentary film, *Always in Season,* founder of Black Vegans Rock, and owner of ARJSV Products, LLC

Aph Ko is twenty-seven years old and lives in Florida. She is the co-author (along with her sister, Syl) of the book, *Aphro-ism: Essays on Pop Culture, Feminism, and Black Veganism from Two Sisters* (2017, Lantern Books). She enjoys cooking vegan food, drinking tea, and watching reality TV while pretending to be a revolutionary.

Syl Ko, independent researcher

Syl Ko is an independent researcher based in Philadelphia, PA. She is also an avid music collector, animal lover, and (secret) fiction writer.

Amelia M. Kraehe, Assistant Professor of Art Education, University of North Texas

Amelia M. Kraehe is a scholar, mentor, wife, and mom. She was raised by a Black mother and white father, attended an elite women's college as an undergraduate, and later married into a working-class immigrant family. This multifaceted biographical prism shapes her academic interest in better understanding structural and cultural forms of inequality in the arts and education, and her commitment to working with public schools and art museums to develop the capacity for social justice.

Nancy López, Associate Professor of Sociology, University of New Mexico

Nancy López is the daughter of Dominican immigrants who were only able to attend primary school through the second grade. She was born in the Lower East Side of Manhattan and was raised in Baruch Public Houses. Spanish is Nancy's first language. In 1987, she graduated from Washington Irving H.S., a *de facto* racially segregated large public vocational high school for girls. Nancy is privileged to be the mother of two brave young women. She is grateful for the support of her husband and life partner over the last two decades.

Valerie Martinez-Ebers, Political Science professor, University of North Texas

Valerie Martinez-Ebers is a proud Latina of Mexican descent. She studies and writes about Latina/o leadership as well as their mass political behavior and public opinion. Her favorite classes to teach are Latino Politics and The Politics of Rock-n-Roll.

Tayler J. Mathews, PhD student in Political Science, Clark Atlanta University

Tayler J. Mathews is a scholar and an activist whose efforts center on women, gender, and sexuality. Tayler has organized with campus and local collectives around issues such as racial and economic justice, reproductive justice, campus sexual violence, street harassment, and other forms of gender-based violence.

Alta Mauro, Spiritual Life & Intercultural Education, New York University–Abu Dhabi

Alta Mauro is the founding director of Spiritual Life & Intercultural Education at New York University–Abu Dhabi where she leads university efforts related to student, staff, and faculty intercultural competence. She finds doing cultural work in the heart of the Middle East both challenging and exciting; it provides a unique backdrop for her to consider what it means to be a wife, mother, daughter, sister, and homegirl, educating from the intersection of Black, critical, and womanist perspectives. Alta earned a PhD in Educational Leadership and Cultural Foundations from the University of North Carolina at Greensboro. Her research focuses on shifting notions of self and identity among upwardly mobile African-American women.

Robin Zape-tah-hol-ah Starr Minthorn, Assistant Professor in Educational Leadership and Native American Studies, University of New Mexico

Robin Starr Zape-tah-hol-ah Minthorn is a citizen of the Kiowa Tribe of Oklahoma and a descendant of the Umatilla, Nez Perce, Assiniboine, and Apache tribes. She is a mother, daughter, partner, sister, auntie and embodies the roles gifted to her by the Creator. Her work strives to honor the ancestors and Indigenous scholars who have come before her. Robin hopes that we all walk in love and beauty in our bravery in the academy and our communities.

Yolanda Flores Niemann, Professor of Psychology, University of North Texas

Yolanda Flores Niemann identifies as a *Tejana* and Mexican-American heterosexual cisgender woman. She is the first in her family of origin to be formally educated beyond middle school. She and her husband of forty years, Barry Niemann, treasure the time they spend with their son, daughter, grandchildren, and extended family members. Yolanda looks forward to many more years as a psychology professor whose teaching, research, and service center on social justice, equity, and the intersections among race, sex, social class, and gender identity for understanding tokenized contexts in higher education.

Mariela Nuñez-Janes, Associate Professor of Anthropology, University of North Texas

Mariela Nuñez-Janes also known as "profe" by students and youth activists, is a 1.5-generation Latina immigrant anthropologist, mother, and partner to her husband. She grew up in Maracaibo with her Puerto Rican mother and Venezuelan father and migrated to the US at the age of thirteen. She was raised by her older sister while her parents worked hard to support their family in their new homeland. Her personal experiences with migration, diaspora, and structural violence anchor her pedagogical and research interests in migrant families and undocumented youth and her commitment to working with vulnerable communities towards freedom and social justice.

Archana A. Pathak, Assistant Professor of Gender, Sexuality, & Women's Studies, Virginia Commonwealth University

Archana A. Pathak is a 1.5er South Asian Indian-American diasporic woman who is the daughter of immigrants. Born into an upper-class, upper-caste family, she was brought to the United States at the age of four by her parents. She identifies as a Hindu, middle-class/bourgeois, queer, able-bodied, cisgender, femme for whom the relentless pursuit of social justice has been the focal light that has guided her professional career. It has also deeply shaped her personal life, at times in painful ways.

Natanya A. Pulley, Assistant Professor of English, Colorado College

Natanya Ann Pulley is a Diné (Navajo) writer and writes mostly fiction and creative non-fiction. Natanya's research, teaching, and writing interests include: Monster and Horror Theory, Narrative Theory and Disability Theory, and graphic novels, which means she spends her time thinking about monsters, societal fears, and abjection, how time shapes narrative, liminal voices, and broken forms, how the body is made weird by expectations of normalcy, and comics. Her writing and editorial work can be found on her website (gappsbasement.com), while she can be found nestled against the eastern foot of the Rocky Mountains in Colorado Springs with her husband and two rowdy dogs.

Nelli Sargsyan, Assistant Professor of Anthropology, Marlboro College

Nelli Sargsyan is an Armenian cisgender woman from post-Soviet Armenia. Նա consistently killjoys the books նրա family is reading, songs they are listening to, movies or TV shows they are watching. Նա has recently come back to enjoying singing again and is looking forward to a summer of trailer-living on the move.

Andrea Silva, Assistant Professor of Political Science, University of North Texas

Andrea Silva is a California Latina enjoying new adventures in Texas. She enjoys reading comic books about women and people of color and following the activities and opinions of her shero, Supreme Court Justice Sonia Sotomayor.

Janelle M. Silva, Associate Professor of Community Psychology and Society, Ethics & Behavior at the University of Washington, Bothell

Janelle M. Silva is a first-generation Chicanx from Southern California. She grew up wearing her father's "hippie beads" with a "Viva La Raza" button and asking what the boycott grapes bumper sticker meant in the garage. She is grateful for the immeasurable support from her partner, Avenicio E. Baca, III, their three cats, Kimo, Peanut, and Peso, and their new puppy Panchito, as she continues to make waves on campus.

Alessandra Bazo Vienrich, PhD candidate in Sociology, University of Massachusetts Boston

Alessandra Bazo Vienrich was born in Lima, Peru and raised in Kernersville, North Carolina. She is currently a PhD candidate in Sociology at the University of Massachusetts—Boston and benefitted from DACA until 2017. She is passionate about breaking boundaries as a student, researcher, and instructor, and does research on undocumented immigrant college students, and teaches courses on race, ethnicity, and immigration. Alessandra lives in Boston, Massachusetts with her husband, Robert.

Bianca C. Williams, Associate Professor of Anthropology, The Graduate Center, CUNY

Bianca C. Williams is a first-generation college-educated, New York-born, Florida-raised, Black heterosexual Christian cisgender woman, who is Jamaican everywhere and always. Committed to helping Black folx be affirmed and emotionally well in their fight for Black liberation, her research interests include Black women and happiness; race, gender, and emotional labor in higher education; feminist pedagogies; and, Black feminist leadership studies. Bianca truly believes in the potential of anthropology and the academy to make social change, which means she is also frequently a radically honest critic of the two. (It's all love.) When she's trying to reenergize and replenish, you can catch Bianca reading, going to theater, consuming film and music, most likely near the ocean, on her own and with loved ones.

Manya C. Whitaker, Assistant Professor of Education, Colorado College

Manya Whitaker is a third-generation teacher who is proud to uphold the ethos of "lifting as we climb" in the Black community. To combat the depth of educational inequality within communities of color, she started an educational consulting business (Blueprint Educational Strategies) to provide income-based academic counseling to families, as well as teacher workshops for urban schools. Although she no longer maintains her blog on diversity and equity in education (theotherclass.wordpress.com), she continues her conversation about educational equity in her role as school board member for a K-12 charter school. When she isn't reading, writing, or teaching about urban education, she likes to sit on her deck, read romance novels, and enjoy the Colorado mountain view. Manya is careful to balance the chaos and stress of academic life with exercise, horseback riding, and plenty of reality TV.

Index

Blackwell, Maylei 95
Black women 146–147; faculty x, 18–23, 58–60, 71, 118–123; graduate students 18–19; intellectual activism xv; leaving academia 51–57; professional development 79–90; sexual violence and 44; tears of 118–123
Black Women's Initiative 72, 78
bodies, pregnant and nursing 137–145
boundaries 61, 104, 121, 126, 128
bravery xi–xvi, 1–4, 12–16, 44, 66; appearance and 91; brutality and 69; "coming out" as undocumented 130, 133–134; communal 107–114; confronting sexual harassment 49–50; Indigenous 25–32; in leaving academia 51, 54–58; motherhood and 138–145; tears and 118–123; *see also* courage; vulnerability
Butler, Anthea xv
But Some of Us Are Brave (Hull, Scott & Smith) xii, 1

canon 152
capital: access to 84; liberation 39; transformational intersectional 39–41
capitalism 112
career calling 58–66
Castañeda, Maria 137
Castro, Fatimah Williams xv
celebration x–xvi, 1, 4
Census (2020) 36
Chicana feminism 7–16; *see also* Xicana feminism
children 137–145
Childs, John Brown 98
Chipaumire, Nora 150
citations 30, 160n1
citizenship 40, 135n5
civil rights 43–44, 46, 49
class, social 7, 137
classism 1, 8, 14; *see also* discrimination
class privilege 111
classrooms: collective action projects 98–105; as transformative space 100
coaches 85–86
collaboration 30, 98–100
collective resistance 69–114
Collins, Patricia Hill xv, 33, 39–40
colonization 28, 54, 56; from feminist position 107, 111–114; *see also* decolonization

color-blind racism 7–12
color line 36
comadrazgo 95–96
comadres 95
"coming out": as undocumented 130, 133–134
communal care 107–114
communal healing 111
communities: Black 52, 55, 57, 64–65; campus 47; classrooms as 98–100; Indigenous 25–32, 34–35, 92, 156; marginalized xi, 102, 149–150; partnerships with 64–65; work-life balance and 103–105
community college 65–66
compañerismo 72
composure 125
Computer Clubhouse, The 83
Conditionally Accepted blog (Grollman) xii; *see also Inside Higher Ed*
confidence 126
conformity 1, 125; *see also* norms, academic
conversations xiv, 33, 112–113; "kitchen table" 51–57
Cooper, Brittney xv
courage 2, 7, 91–96, 107; *see also* bravery; vulnerability
Cox-Grollman, Cynthia xv
creative writing 124, 127–128
creativity 109–110, 122
critical race feminism 2–3
critical race theory 2–3, 7–8, 34, 37
cross-disciplinarity 23, 113
Cruz, Celia 70
crying 77, 118–123, 127–128
cultural barriers 138
cultural competency 81–82, 84, 86–87
cultural traditions 138–139
curriculum: collective activism projects 98–105; on gender violence 93; race and social justice 37; sociology 62; *see also* academic programs; disciplines, academic

decolonization 54, 102, 113, 149–150; *see also* colonization
Deferred Action for Childhood Arrivals (DACA) 130–131, 135n2, 135n4
dehumanization 121; *see also* humanity
deportation 131, 135n2
Desiderata 146–147